MAYAN CULTURE

Basic Facts

to [illegible]! Merry Christmas 1997 from [illegible] and [illegible]

MAYAN CULTURE

Basic Facts

PANORAMA EDITORIAL

Cover:
Jaina Figure:
Photograph: Enrique Franco Torrijos
Indian from Altos de Chiapas:
Photograph: Ruth D. Lechuga
Mask of the god Chac. Uxmal:
Photograph: Walter Reuter

Text:
Fernando Medina Ruiz

First edition in english: 1985
Fifth reprint: 1991

Leibnitz 31, Col. Anzures
11590 México, D.F.

Translated by:
Gillian Glass

Photographs:
Enrique Franco Torrijos
Ruth D. Lechuga
Walter Reuter
Irmgard Groth
I.N.A.H.

Printed in México
Impreso en México
ISBN 968-38-0144-7

Index

Geography

"Art, the product of man's creative activities, has a very important role to play in our everyday lives. Moreover, it forms an important aspect of our existence providing a subject worthy of deep study not only as regards the great beauty to be found within its various modes of expression but also in terms of man's praiseworthy attempts at its elevation and the effects these attempts have had on the shaping of culture itself." Quotation from Carlos Samayoa Chinchilla.

Records of Mayan history date back to the fourth century A.D. when the Indians of ancient times carved inscriptions on stone monuments and the culture of these peoples continues to harbour misteries enough to capture the interest of those who choose to study this field.

Homogenous cultures appeared, prospered and declined in Mesoamerica, Guatemala, Mexico, Honduras and El Salvador as far north as the Yaqui and Mayo valleys which lie either side of the Panuco river down to the mid-way point in Central America long before the Europeans set foot on the American continent.

The area inhabited by tribes of Mayan Indians covered what we now know as Guatemala, the west of El Salvador and Honduras, Belize and the states of Quintana Roo, Yucatan, Campeche, part of Tabasco and east Chiapas. From maps, we can see that these areas roughly form a quadrangle the north-south side of which measures approximately 900 kilometers. The base of the quadrant forms the

The Mayans occupied a vast territory which nowadays forms part of Mexico, Guatemala, Honduras, Belize and El Salvador. Highrelief from the base of stele 1 at Bonampak, Chiapas, Mexico.

Large settlements and religious centers were built close to cenotes, which were natural underground caverns full of water. The sacred cenote at Chichén Itzá, Yucatán, Mexico.

widest part measuring some 500 kilometers, and the top which forms the northern limit of the Yucatán peninsula, runs over a distance of approximately 400 kilometers.

The quadrangle divides naturally into three sections the first of which comprises the mountain ranges and plateaux of northern Central America. The second part encompasses the plains of El Petén in the north of Guatemala which stretch to the base of the quadrangle in the south of the Yucatán peninsula. Finally, the third section comprises the flatlands of limestone which cover almost all the northern part of the peninsula.

It is very probable that the Mayans were the first to recognize the value of corn as a primary foodstuff and to develop effective methods for its cultivation in the fertile valleys to be found in the west and north of Guatemala during the second and third centuries B.C. From the **Popol Vuh** which has proved to be a unique source of information on indigenous life, we learn that this grain of grains formed an essential part of Man himself. This came to be when the Creator's attempts to breathe life into wood which was too rigid and proved inadequate to call upon the gods, and clay which was too crumbly, failed.

On the high plateaux of Guatemala, there are two large lakes formed by volcanic activity called Amatitlán and Atitlán. Linked to the Bay of Amatique by the Golfete and Dulce rivers lies the lake of Izabal. Lake Guaja is situated between Guatemala and El Salvador and to its east lies another lake called Ayarza. In the area of El Petén, there are over one hundred inland expanses of water the largest of which is the Petén-Itzá, formerly known as the Chahaltunhá.

Various waterways flow into the Gulf of Mexico the Motagua which flows from El Quiché to the Bay of Honduras (Bay of Omoa) and the Usumacinta into which flow the rivers Negro or Chixoy, Salinas, La Pasión and others.

Rising in the west in the Cuchumatán mountains, flow the Selegua river (in Mexico this river is called the Río Grande de Chiapas) and the Grijalva river. These rivers flow into the sea along the Gulf coast. It is presumed that the rivers in El Petén along with the rivers Mopán, Sarstún, Río Azul or Hondo river, and the Moho which flow through Belize constituted the major waterways of the Classic Mayan Period. They form a semi-circle which leads historians to conclude that they certainly must have aided communication between the West Indies and the Gulf of Mexico down to the south of the Yucatán peninsula.

Corn, beans, rice, potatoes, pumpkins, cassava (which according to Rafael Girard grew out of human remains and the cultivation of which preceeded cereal production), chayote, yams and calabash are all well-suited for cultivation in the area. Fruit-bearing trees such as the wild cherry, paw-paw, soursop and guava grow in abundance alongside other trees valued for their timber used in construction work. Other trees have medicinal properties or produce natural dyes.

Like the magical flora of the area, there is a wider variety of fauna to be found on the scorched lowlands than on the uplands. Wildlife features jaguars, or American tigers, pumas, lions, elks, wild boar, walruses, monkeys, snakes, lizards, chelonians, deer and small mammals. Some are the friends of Man whilst others are his enemies. Birdlife ranges from the caudal eagle to the humming bird and many species of butterfly are noteworthy in the insect world. The Quetzal is considered by the Mayans to be the representative of the gods flying high over the mountains of Chiapas, the hils of Chamá and Chuacús in the Verapaces of Guatemala as well as over the highlands of El Petén.

The plains of El Petén and the hills which surround them stretching to Mediodía are only about 150 meters above

The lagoon at Najá in Chiapas, Mexico. Jungle, rivers and lakes are to be found in the region comprising the Mayan world.

sea level. From east to west, a range of mountains called the Mayan Mountains extend for a distance of 100 kilometers. In the foothills of these mountains lie fifteen lakes, several of which join up and run into each other during periods of heavy rainfall. The Itzae indians migrated towards the Yucatán peninsula leaving behind the shores of the largest lake in this region, the Petén-Itza. They later returned to their former watery home-lands at the time of the internal conflicts (including the break-down of the Mayapán League) which preceeded the Conquest.

Nowadays, the natural communication system provided by the rivers has broken down for long stretches due to the encroachment of the jungle and swamplands. The system rises in Laguna de Términos, the estuaries of the Grijalva and in the Usumacinta which are situated in the gulf area and which wend their ways to the coastlines of Guatemala and Honduras. The southern tip of the arc lies in the great Gulf of Mexico itself. In the north of the Yucatán peninsula, there are no superficial expanses of water. There are, however, large wells formed by underground currents which open to the surface and are known as **cenotes**.

The homelands of the Mayans of the Classical Period stretch south, east and west of El Petén, Palenque, Bonam-

pak and Yaxchilán (nowadays called Chiapas, Mexico) which are as typically Mayan as Altar de Sacrificios, Uaxactún, Seibal, Cancúen and Quiriguá in Guatemala and Copán in Honduras.

It is possible that this vast region was abandoned due to water shortages during the dry season. Excavations and fragments of pottery which have been uncovered indicate that the area was inhabited by human beings from the Prehistoric Period until the end of the Classic Period when the Mayans journeyed to settle in the central part of the Yucatán peninsula.

The area of El Petén is mainly composed of dense, overgrown jungle through which rivers cleave their way fed by underground rivers and channels the water levels of which rise and fall in accordance with the rainfall. These rivers run into the Usumacinta in the west which in turn flows into the Gulf of Mexico. The rivers Holmul, Mopán, Sarstún and Río Hondo flow in the opposite direction and meet the sea at the Caribbean Whilst smaller lakes and lagoons dry up and disappear during the dry season others become swamps or their water levels drop drastically. As a result, conditions for cultivating crops are difficult in approximately one third of El Petén which explains the tough battle for survival waged by the Mayan peoples.

After a heavy wet season, marshes and swamps are as frequent as areas of dry land. Both human and animal life alike were dependant on the "rains" for survival and as a result the great archaeological ruins at Tikal, Uaxactún, El Naranjo, Nakum, Yaxhá, Holmul, Chunhuitz, Benque Viejo and Xinantunich in Belize, San Clemente, Naachtún (on the border with Campeche), La Honradez and many others are situated close to **chultunes** or underground caverns created for the purpose of storing water collected during the rainy season. At several sites, remains of primitive irrigation systems have been uncovered such as those which can be seen at Etzná and Kohunlich.

It is amazing to consider how the early Mayans managed to live and reach such levels of development given their distinct lack, or excess, of water along with the lack of any real positive agricultural stimuli.

The flora of the second section of the Mayan world is dispersed over open grasslands and dense jungle. Commonly found trees include the kapok tree (also called the **yaxché**) which was sacred to the ancient Mayans. The bark of the amate tree was used to make a type of paper for "writing" and painting on. The sapodilla was valued for the extremely hard timber that it yields and which was commonly used for construction purposes as well as for providing gum. The timber of this tree was used for the lintels of the great temples at Tikal (Temple number 4, or the

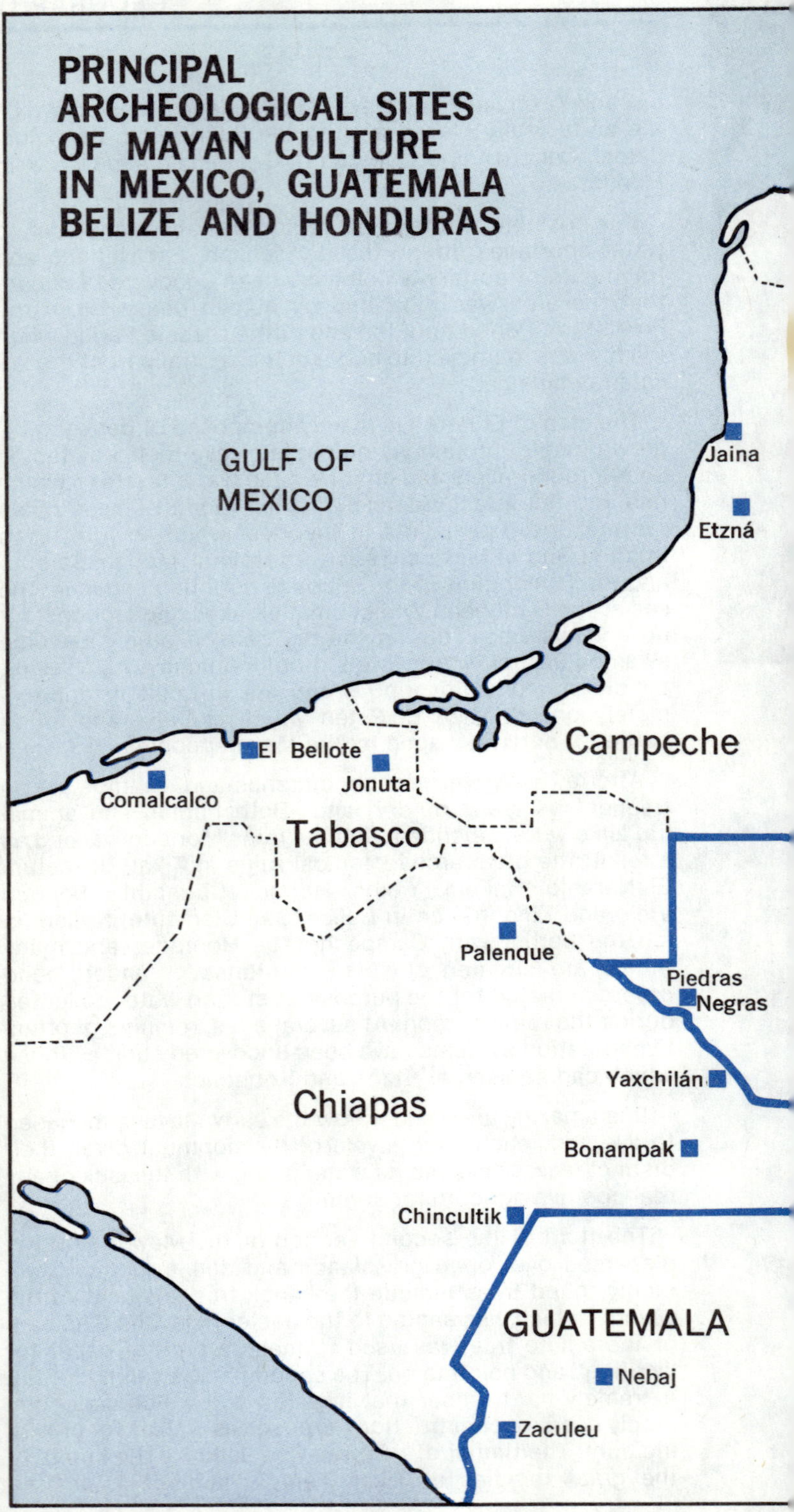
PRINCIPAL
ARCHEOLOGICAL SITES
OF MAYAN CULTURE
IN MEXICO, GUATEMALA
BELIZE AND HONDURAS
GULF OF
MEXICO
Jaina
Etzná
Campeche
El Bellote
Jonuta
Comalcalco
Tabasco
Palenque
Piedras
Negras
Yaxchilán
Chiapas
Bonampak
Chincultik
GUATEMALA
Nebaj
Zaculeu

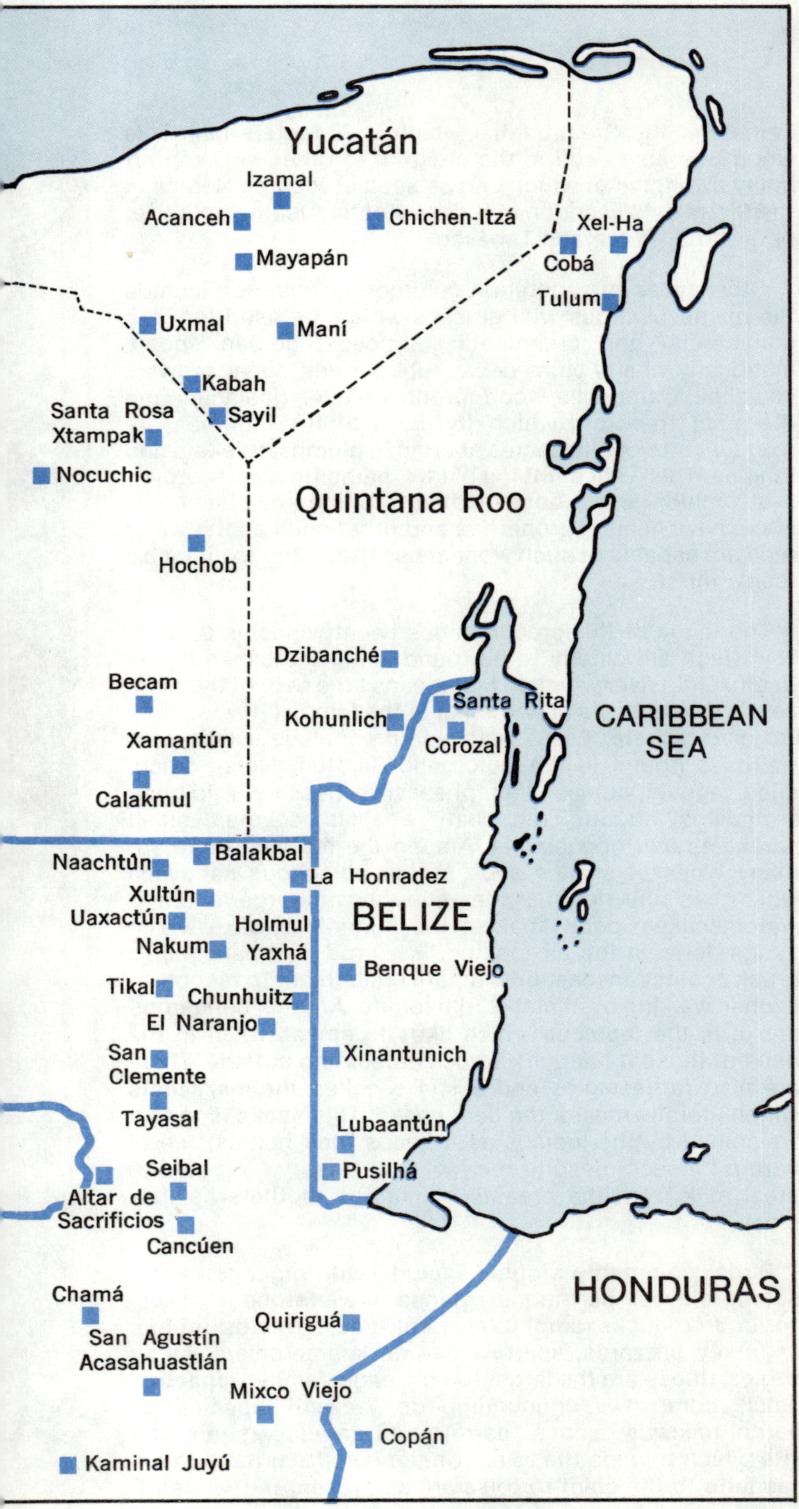
Yucatán
Izamal
Acanceh
Chichen-Itzá
Xel-Ha
Cobá
Mayapán
Tulum
Uxmal
Maní
Kabah
Santa Rosa
Xtampak
Sayil
Nocuchic
Quintana Roo
Hochob
Dzibanché
Becam
Santa Rita
Kohunlich
CARIBBEAN
SEA
Corozal
Xamantún
Calakmul
Balakbal
Naachtún
La Honradez
Xultún
BELIZE
Uaxactún
Holmul
Nakum
Yaxhá
Benque Viejo
Tikal
Chunhuitz
El Naranjo
Xinantunich
San
Clemente
Tayasal
Lubaantún
Seibal
Pusilhá
Altar de
Sacrificios
Cancúen
HONDURAS
Chamá
Quiriguá
San Agustín
Acasahuastlán
Mixco Viejo
Copán
Kaminal Juyú

Temple of the Great Jaguar which is 70 meters tall). This wood was also used in the creation of other works of art many examples of which can be seen at Piedras Negras in the Sierra del Lacandón at the apex of the Usumacinta river between El Petén and Tabasco.

Other types of vegetation common to this area include the mamey, various wild grasses which are used for both commercial and ornamental purposes, golden spoon, mahogany, cherry plum, cedar, rubber trees, copal, browse, cowslips, Campeche wood (produces dye), guaiacum and the quira tree from which the keys of the marimba are made. Plants of all species abound in clumps, thickets and tangles. There are climbing plants, parasitic plants, crow's foot orchids and a host of others. Some are poisonous, some have healing properties and other such as the water reed are capable of such wonders as the ability to quench a man's thirst.

The fauna of this area includes twenty species of monkey which are chiefly to be found along the banks of the Usumacinta river which in fact means "the river of the monkeys". One species in particular is the famous howler monker or **zaraguate**. Lesser pachyderms include elks, tapirs, walruses (found in the Dulce and Sarstún rivers), crocodiles, jaguars, pumas, deer, pheasants, peccary, wild boar, armadillos, agoutis, red coati, weasels, coyotes, small parakeets and oppossums. Among the reptiles, there are many types of snakes such as the poisonous **nahuyaca** which has four nostrils; the yellow beard; large land and water snakes; coral snakes; the humming snake which hangs down in the air looking like a rod. If it happens to brush against anyone unfortunate enough not to recognize it when walking by, it marks him for life. Another dangerous snake is the **tepolcúa** which likes to embed itself in the anus of those it happens across defecating outside. There are also rattlesnakes and a snake called the **mazacuata** which literally means the deer snake. This snake is in fact welcomed by the Indians as it keeps their homes free of harmful insects despite the fact that it is also reputed to steal milk from the breasts of nursing mothers as they sleep.

Birds commonly sighted include wild pigeons, softly cooing doves, partridges, guinea fowl, stone curlews, coots, tree ducks (amphibians), vultures, buzzards, urubus or turkey buzzards, sparrow hawks, lammergeiers, harpy eagles, (these are the largest of the eagle family), **gipaetos**, quail, curassows, hummingbirds, several species of heron, macaws, tucans, parrots and paraqueets, and the kite which heralds the rains. Chelonians from the humble **casquito** to the giant tortoise are all present in the area.

The Kapok tree was sacred to the Mayans.

Representatives of the saurian family are lizards, crocodiles and allgators and tropical lizards. Fish of all types from the delicious red snapper to the **guapote**, sole and spiny loach are present. (The eggs of the loach are considered to be the "caviar of America".) The existence of crustaceans and molluscs is already recorded in the **Popol Vuh** since it was a large crab which caused the downfall of Zipacná, the rival of the heroes Hunahpú and Ixbalanqué.

The dry, lowlying plains of northern Yucatán (which rise from a height of 30 meters to 180 meters above sea level) in the third section of the quadrangle are almost devoid of vegetation and wildlife. Along the Levantine coast, there are palms and palmettos, pheasant and deer which are the symbols of the Mayab. Towards the north-eastern corner (Quintana Roo), the jungle reappears and provides a backdrop to Tulum.

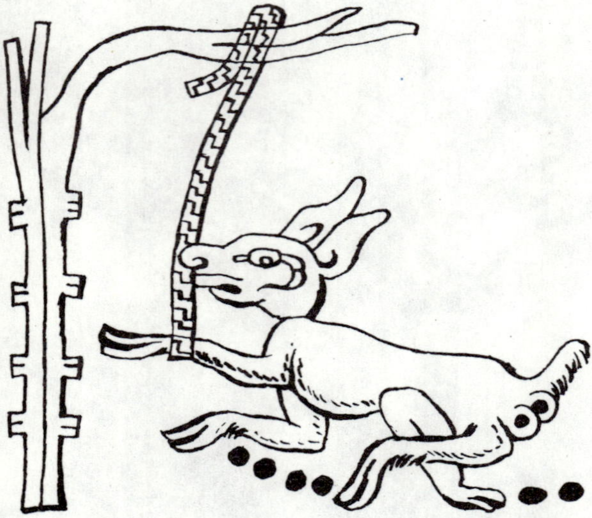

A captured stag. The Trocortesian Codex. National Library of Madrid.

In the northern half of the area, ground vegetation is sparse and the region lacks water sources. The largest espanse of water to be found inland is the lake of Bacalar, Quintana Roo. Also worthy of mention is the cove of Xel-Ha, also in Quintana Roo. Most of the drinking water consumed in this area is provided by the **cenotes** which are wells formed by shifts in the lime strata caused by underground currents.

This region which has been the home of the Mayan peoples since times long past, was the place where their great culture was reborn and to which was added the great wealth of the Toltecs during the eleventh and twelfth centuries A.D. as well as along the eastern coast and the north-south axis.

During the Classic Period (350-900 A.D.), the Mayans made contact with the Zapotec civilization (influenced by the Mayans), the people of Teotihuacán (also influenced by the Mayans), as well as with the Olmecs and the Totonac-Huasteca indians from El Tajin, Veracruz. Thus, the Mayans extended the influence of their knowledge during their migrations around the Gulf area (center and south Mexico) as far north as the Pánuco river.

The effect of coming into contact with the Mayans on other civilizations varied considerably and in return, the

The jaguar was always present in the lives of the Mayans. Reliefs from a stele at Tikal, Guatemala.

Hemp was grown all over the vast plain of the Yucatán.

Mayans were also influenced by meeting other migratory communities— the influence of the Toltecs is particularly relevant as regards the Mayans of the Yucatán.

Some historians reject the theory that the Mayan peoples emerged and kept themselves very much to themselves, isolating themselves in the middle of the New World. On the other hand, some scholars believe that the culture of the Mayans is autochtonous, born in the area without knowledge of or links with any other "imported" civilization.

History

During the second and third centuries A.D. a civilization appeared and burgeoned in Mesoamerica, refining and bringing together the elements which formed their heritage and thus created one of the most famous cultures the world has ever seen. Over a period of six or seven centuries known as the Classic Period, the Mayans executed a great intellectual feat, erecting monumental stone structures which have inspired awe throughout the world. They carried out research in the fields of astronomy and the measuring of time. using a form of writing not unsimilar to the phonetic system, they laid down their thoughts and beliefs for posterity and finally, it is to these people that we owe the credit for "inventing" the number zero which had not been used by any other civilization prior to theirs.

Mayan chronology starts with the Pre-classic Horizon which according to some researchers occured around 3000 B.C. Others, however determine the dates for this period to be between 600 B.C. and 200 A.D. The Classic Period which is also known as the Old Empire lasted from 200-900 A.D. and was followed by the Post-classic Period or the New Empire. It was during this final period that the integration of the Mexicas and the Toltecs took place. This period lasted from 900 A.D. until 1500 — tat is until the time of the Conquest.

According to Sylvannus G. Morley, the Mayan civilization was based on agriculture in its later stages. During the early periods, the Indians depended on fishing and foraging for survival. They also hunted large and small game and were the first people to cultivate tubercules.

The chief crop of the Mayans was corn which came originally from the uplands of western Guatemala (**Popol Vuh**) and was a "gift from the Creator." It was discovered growing

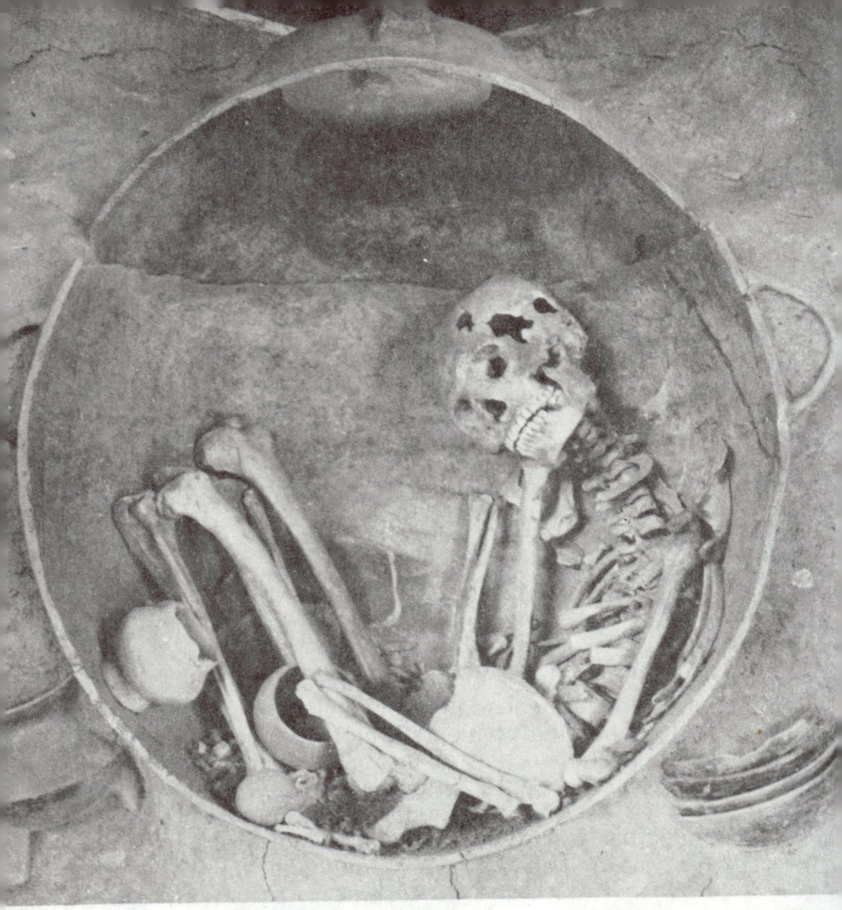

A Mayan funeral in Zaculeu, Guatemala. The body has been placed in a clay urn along with various offerings.

in this area before the Mayan culture came to flourish on the scorched lowlands of El Petén.

Morley himself recommends that the term, "the Mayan civilization" should be applied exclusively to describe the ancient culture which used hieroglyphics, studied the calculation of time and developed novel styles of architecture in stone which included the use of arched ceilings and the invention of the Mayan or False Arch.

Morley divides the Classic Period into two main stages and points out that the name, the Classic Period, has nothing to do with political events and refers only to cultural achievements. "It must be made absolutely clear that the terms Old and New Empire do not imply any political activity whatsoever. On the contrary, they are used exclusively in a cultural and esthetic sense to describe an empire of thougt, language, customs, religious practice and popular artistic activities. The Mayans were a homogenous

Corn, "a gift from the Creator," was the basic foodstuff of the Mayans.

(orthodox) people who enjoyed a common civilization without any political concepts of unity."

Since there is very little reliable information remaining about the Classic Period, it is futile to go into the subject in any greater depth. Historical records from that time were unfortunately destroyed. Even though Spanish chroniclers described events from the twelfth century on (the Postclassic Period), the original records kept by the Indians themselves describing the rising, zenith and sunset of their great culture are lost forever.

Archaeology, however, still provides us with a wealth of information — inscriptions on steles, temples and palaces. Art, architecture, sculptures, paintings and pottery have also left us clues. From the fragments of pottery uncovered by the archaelogists, we can accurately trace the changes in Mayan culture and determine whether they occured because of outside influences or because of the commercial needs of other communities.

Archaeological artifacts, nonetheless, have fallen prey to plundering on an undeterminable scale and a lot of treasures still lie concealed within the ever encroaching jungle.

Thus, the origins of the Mayan people remains shrouded in mystery along with other aspects of their existence. As

CHRONOLOGY OF THE MAYAN

LOWER PENINSULAR PLAIN (Campeche, Yucatan, Quintana Roo)				CENTRAL JUNGLE AREA (Tabasco, Chiapas, Guatemala, Belize, Honduras)	
DATE	PERIOD	CERAMIC &/or ARCHITECTURAL CULTURAL PHASE	PLACES	CERAMIC &/or ARCHITECTURAL CULTURAL PHASE	PLACES
1530	Conquest				
1500					
1400	PCST-CLASSIC Late	Mayapan tribal alliance Izamal is the center of religious power	Mayapan	Tayasal	Tayasal, Guatemala
1300			T'ho Xelhá		Naco, Honduras
1200		Contact with the Mixtecs Xiu or Itzáes Alliance	Sta Rita Cozumel		Itzamkanac
1100	Early	Metallurgu, Chac Mool Maya-Toltec hegemony	Tulum Champoton	Abandon	Acalan Calakmul
1000					Naachtun Palenque
900			Izamal		Piedras Negras, Guatemala
800		Architectural art flourishes	Polé, Xelhá Cobá, Tancáh		Yaxchilan Bonampak
700	CLASSIC Late	Chenes & Puuc	Oxkintok, Acancéh Chichén Itzá	Tepeuh	Xultun Quirigua
600			Etzná, Hochob Uxmal, Kabáh Sayil, Labná		Copan,Honduras Chama
500		Rio Bec style	Xpuhil Rio Bec		Chinkultik
400	Early		Jaina Becan, Yaxuna Sta Rosa Xtampak	Tzakol	Comalcalco Jonuta
300					Tzimin Kax Tonina
200		Acancéh ceramics			
100				Matzanel	
0					Holmul
100	Late		Holactún		El Naranjo
200			Dzibilchaltún	Chicanel	Tikal
300					Seibal
400					Uaxactun
500	Middle			Mamon	Altar de Sacrificios
600					Benque Viejo
700	PRE-CLASSIC	Cenote Maní			
800			Dzibilchaltún		
900					
1000				Xeh	
1100					Cuevas de Copan
1200			Cenote Maní		
1300	Early	Swazey			
1400					
1500					
1600					
1700					

HIGHLANDS OF CHIAPAS AND GUATEMALA		PACIFIC COAST	
CERAMIC &/or ARCHITECTURAL CULTURAL PHASE	PLACES	CERAMIC &/or ARCHITECTURAL CULTURAL PHASE	PLACES
Mixco Viejo	Mixco Viejo Iximché		
Ayampuc		Plumbate	
Amatle			
Pamplona			
Esperanza	Kaminal juyu	Sta Lucia	
		Cotzumalapa	
Aurora	Amatitlan		Jiquizate
Miraflores	Nebaj		
		El Baul	El Baul
Sacatepeques	Zacualpa		
		Conchas	Usulutan
			Abaj Takalik
Las Charcas	Chiapa de Corzo		Izapa
	Padre Piedra		Yarumela
			La Victoria
		Cuadros	
Arévalo			
		Ocos	

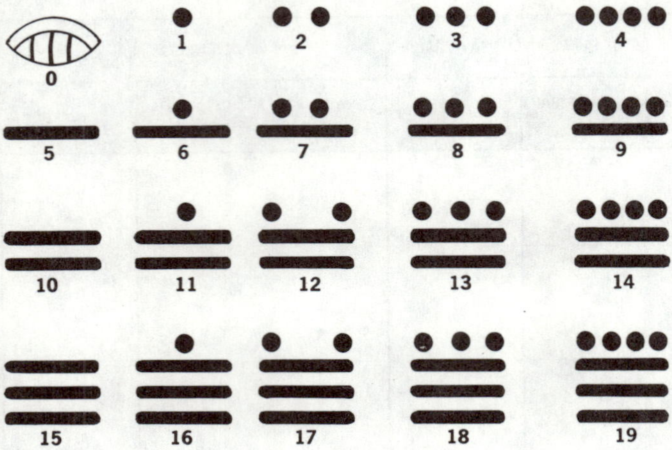

Mayan numerals 0 to 19 in the stick/point system.

we have already mentioned, the reason for the downfall of their empire is not clear. One possible theory would suggest that ground clearance which is a rather barbarous agricultural method still in practice along with the mayans' primitive forms of cultivation led to the cancer which destroyed the land —erosion. As a result, when water levels were low, the waterways became blocked and turned into pools of mud or dried up completely leaving dry beds of silt. Other explanations point to breakdowns in the political system, administrative disorganization, plagues and pests which afflicted both man and earth alike. All these factors were further aggravated by increases in population. Most Mayan experts would agree on this last point and others would add armed invasion and internal disputes, low rainfall, a general decline in health and well-being to our list.

The Classic Period ended in El Petén with the Indians migrating further north to the Yucatán peninsula. There they constructed great cities such as Chichén Itzá. The Post-classic Period dawned. In the Yucatán, the Mayans came into contact with the Mexica Indians who influenced their beliefs, art and customs which led them to make changes in the classical archetypes.

In their new homeland, the Mayans suffered many conflicts and changes in fortune. They also had many moments of triumph and left the indellible mark of their culture in several places as can be seen at Monte Albán, Teotihuacán, Tula and Xochicalco.

Internal disputes brought about a more speedy end to the Mayan world. Desing on Lintel 8, Yaxchilán Chiapas Mexico.

A little later more internal disputes broke out almost as if the gloomy predictions of the books of **Chilam Balam** were bent on becoming destructive truth. The high point of these disputes was the breakdown of the Mayapan League which was an alliance formed among the cities of Uxmal, Chichén Itzá and Mayapán.

The Itzá Mayans who had suffered crushing defeat in 1204 AD against the Cocmames from Mayapán, had to return to the shores of the lake, once again making the difficult journey back. There they lived in peace until the arrival of Urzúa y Arizmendi's troops who took them by storm at their fortress of Tayazal in Chatunhá or Petén-Itzá in 1700.

At the downfall of the Quiché empire which was caused by political unrest precipitated by the Conquest, the sons of Quicab the Great declared that they no longer supported their father and declared war against him which they won. The enraged king subsequently condemned them with the words, "may my curse go with you commoners in the hour of your victory." The curse was fulfilled upon the arrival of the **Teules** who burned the Indian monarchy of **Popol Vuh** to ashes.

When the Spaniards arrived in the Yucatán, the Mayans had long since broken with their former religious and cultural identity.

The Mayans sub-divide into various ethnic and linguistic groups. Chontal indians from Atitlán, Guatemala.

The Mayan Indian

As a rule Mayan men are short in stature rarely measuring more than 1.65 m (5' 3'') in height. A typical face has high cheek bones, a small chin and an aquiline nose. These features are clearly distinguishable on the Palenque masks. The eyes are slanting like those of Mongoloids and are dark in color. Complexion wise, the Indians have smooth, swarthy skins and do not normally have beards, the only exception to this being the Lacandon Indians.

Mayan women are generally shorter than the men. Both men and women are brachcephalic, the Mayans from the Yucatán to a greater extent than their southern brothers. In the south, dolichocephalic skulls have been noted. The metabolic rate of the Mayans is usually between five and eight degrees higher than that of Caucasians. At rest, their pulse is approximately fifty-two beats per minute which is about nine beats slower than the average white man's.

Physically, the Mayans have well-developed muscular legs, broad chests and short necks. Their teeth are small and compact and generally remain good well into old age. In the days of the ancient Mayans, children who were chosen to enter the priesthood had their heads elongated to proclaim their privileged status. Their mothers would put splints on the children's heads shortly after birth to deform the skull. Another sign of privileged position was squinting eyes and to induce this feature, mothers would hang little pebbles from the ends of the hair in front of the eyes. Nowadays, the Mayans continue to look like their forefathers but no longer deform their heads nor find squints quite so appealing!

Mayan psychology bears in mind their traditions, ancestry and dignity which have often suffered great injustices throughoot history.

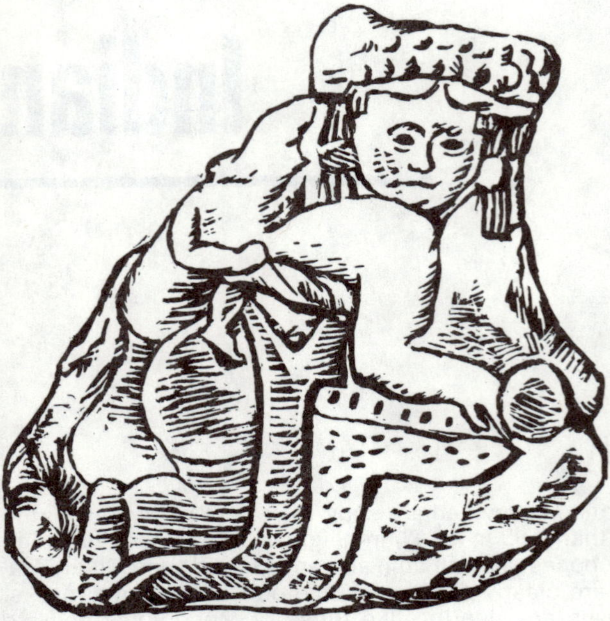

Mayan woman grinding corn in a metate.
From a figurine from Lubaantún, Belize.

Mayan men and women are kind, intelligent people. They are naturally brave but are somewhat reserved in the presence of strangers.

They appear to be allergic to the innovations of the twentieth century, are clean, modest, humble and faithful to their splendid past history during which they proved to be considerate and respectful of the rights of others and as brave as young tigers during their magnificent battles.

To this day, all Mayans continue to hold very high moral values and these are expressed in the sad, solemn spiritual music from Yucatán and the uplands of Guatemala.

Personal hygiene has always been very important for the Mayans. They wash themselves as if performing a rite at home both before and after work maintaining that cleanliness brings rest and purity of body and soul.

Although they wander and disappear in a world which they are unable to love because it confuses them, they possess a keen sense of community spirit and on the whole are pleasant people. They rarely lie or deceive others wittingly even out of self-interest or fear. Their stoicism and resigna-

Tzontziles from San Andrés
Larraizar, Chiapas, Mexico.

tion towards change is admirable. They prefer to suffer and die without lament in the knowledge that a better world awaits them when they eventually return to the home of the Creator and that their memory will remain on earth as the memory of those superior beings from whom they received the code for life, remains.

Their comedown, however, is that they are a very superstitious people in spite of being sheep in the fold of Christ. Often they mix sacred rites with pagan ceremonies — in many instances, when praying before the images of saints surrounded by animals, their petitions are addressed to the lesser beings! Nowadays, in the heart of the mountains, they still worship old idols such as Tohil, Avilix and Pascual Abaj. These are the gods of the Santa Cruz area of El Quiché and Chichicastenango. Humans are no longer offered up to the gods as sacrifices to ensure light, heat, rain, better harvests and a life without tribulation; instead, they now make offerings of the first fruits of the countryside, animals and, at times, their own blood. Those who are not knowledgeable in their ways or outsiders are not permited to take part in their liturgies which mainly take place at night.

The Mayans are generally fatalistic and lack a developed sense of initiative. They are passive people who prefer to spectate rather than play an active role in the drama of mankind.

They Mayans of today, like those of the past, are thrifty. Their basic diet consists of corn **tortillas**, beans and chiles supplemented with game or fish. Thus fed, they carry out

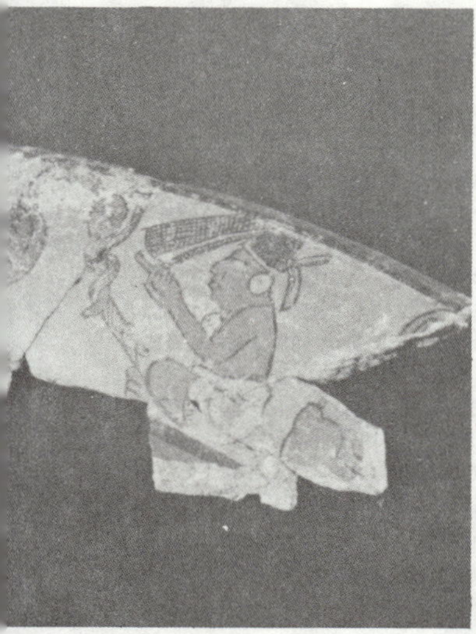

One of the rare examples of Mayan erotic art can be appreciated on this fragment of a plate found in Uaxactún. La Aurora Museum, Guatemala City.

their duties in the fields, make long treks, and live their lives in wretched conditions. Lechery is almost unknown to them: the Institute of Anthropology and History in Guatemala has only one piece depicting anything of this nature — a multicolored plate showing a monkey carressing a woman's breasts.

Pieces depicting phalluses were found in the Olmec settlements on the southern coast of Guatemala in La Democracia, El Baúl, and Chichén Itzá. These howeves, do not stern from Mayan culture.

Mayans are naïve people who hold on to their traditions. They show respect for their elderly and support their children, womenfolk and the infirm. They tend to be quiet and introverted, not given to showy displays of behavior. They work hard, live peaceably, are home-lovers and show great affection for domestic animals.

The theory that the Mayans may have asiatic origins is upheld by some of their physical characteristics: the epicanthic fold in their eyes, the Mongolian patch which disappears at puberty, and the lines on the palms of their hands.

It is estimated that there are approximately four million Mayan Indians who are mainly distributed over the areas of Mexico and Guatemala. The various tribes are the Quichés, Chakchiqueles, Quekchies, Itzaes, Zutuhiles, Chamulas, Mames, Pokomames, Chabañales, Zoques, Choles, Tzendales, Tzotziles, Pokomchies, Mopanes, Chortís, Chontales, Lacandones, Tojolabales, etc. These tribes each posess their own Mayan language or language derived from Mayan, the principal forms of which are Quiché and Yucatecan.

Despite their poor living conditions, the Mayan population is on the increase (except among the Lacandons who are dying out principally because of hemophilia which is fostered by the practice of intermarrying). They also suffer other endemic diseases but have not yet yielded to the pressures of civilization as we know it. Their settlements are to be found along both banks of the Usumacinta (the right bank is in Guatemala and the left bank in Mexico) in an area which commences at the Lacantún river in Chiapas and stretches south to the Lacandon Mountains. The north is bordered by El Petén, Chiapas and Tabasco.

Normally, women are about sixteen or seventeen when they have their first child. Mayan woman are fertile, loving mothers and make unselfish wives.

According to Sylvannus G. Morley, the Ancient Mayan Empire extended linguistically in a northward direction where the Mayan language developed into **Itzá** (which is still spoken by the Indians of the great lake today), **Mopán** (the name of the river rising in El Petén which wends its way to Belize and flows into the Caribbean), as well as other Mayan languages which are still spoken such as **Icainché**, **Lacandón** and the form of Mayan spoken in the Yucatán. In Mérida, Lacandón Indians who had come to sell arrows for hunting deer were heard speaking a language similar to the variation of Mayan spoken in the Yucatàn and consequently were understood by their counterparts.

Mayan also extended southwards being expressed in **Chol**, **Chortí**, **Tzendal**, **Zotzil** and **Chontal**. The area where these are spoken is enormous and stretches from west Honduras to the state of Tabasco, and from there to the uplands of Chiapas.

As Alfred M. Tozzer points out: "The unity of the Mayan-speaking people is admirable "considering that the groups of Náhuatl speakers are scattered all along the Pacific coast of Central America. It would appear that the Mayans were quite happy to settle in one place and obviously not used to moving far from their natural habitat. Furthermore, research does not indicate that there was much communication between the various tribes occupying the relatively small portion of territory in their possession".

"From the times of the oldest Spanish records until present times, most of the Mayan dialects appear to be identified with specific places. There do not seem to have been such great shifts in population as one would have naturally expected."

Lacandón Indian from Chiapas, Mexico.

"Geographical circumstances are perhaps related to this apparent lack of mixing of people of one dialect with those of another. Relatively speaking, the Yucatán peninsula is isolated from the rest of Mayan territory and the language spoken there has undergone very few changes. So few, in fact, that it is possible to compare and judge the language of today with what we know of the language described in the earliest written records available. Communication was rendered difficult given the mountains separating the idiomatic characteristics of the various Mayan dialects."

"The Mayan language is polysynthetic in that the pronominal subjects of the verb are always expressed. In general, it follows the same methods of expression as the majority of the other American languages. As regards lexicography, it differs from all other languages spoken in Mexico and Central America. Some writers claim that the Zapotec language is a closer relative of Mayan than Náhuatl. Studies show, however, that Mayan is morphologically different from Zapoteca."

A modern day woman from Yucatán Mexico.

With their quiet, easy-going manner, the Mayans remain very attached to the ways of their ancestors as regards life and thought. They appear to accept strange customs naturally although they also adhere closely to their own. Deaf and blind to "progress", they defend their own lifestyle with admirable fervor and mystery. It would be truer to say that the white man has assimilated ideas and attitudes from the Mayans rather than the reverse and given this, it is understandable why the Mayan language has not evolved to the extent that Spanish has. Instead, it has influenced morphology, syntaxis and the phonetic structures of spoken Spanish in places where the people were, are, and will continue to be singularly Mayan.

Writing and Literature

Alongside the oral traditions of telling stories, myths, the giving of advice and the casting of spells, there were three principal sources of written literature in the pre-Columbian world. Firstly, the Mayans painted, wrote codices and carved inscriptions. These all served the purpose of recording Mayan news, chronicles and documentary information laid down by the descendants of the ancient Americans following the Conquest. We also learn a considerable amount from the writings and letters of Diego de Landa, the first Bishop of Yucatán; Bernardino de Sahagún; Diego López de Cogolludo; Bernal Díaz del Castillo; Hernán Cortés; Pedro de Alvarado; Antonio de Remesal; Francisco Ximénez; Bartolomé de Las Casas; Francisco de Fuentes and several others.

The Mayans "wrote" several codices using a type of paper made from vegetable fiber called **amate** (the Mayan equivalent of papyrus). They also used specially treated deer skin. "Writing" consisted of ideographs which were painted with a brush. By means of these pictorial records, we learn of their history, art, literature, chronological systems, botany, medicine, religion, astronomy and everything that was both pleasant and painful for Mayan man. Unfortunately for the following generations most of these "painted books" were destroyed during the Conquest. Only three codices survived and they are known as the Dresden Codex which is to be found in the German city of Dresden, the Parisian Codex and the Madrid (or Trocortesian) Codex.

The Dresden Codex, which dates from the Classic Period (200-900 AD) is about astronomy, religion and divination. It is the smallest of all the codices found — its pages are 20cm long by 9cm wide and are broken up into sections by red lines which indicate the start and finish of chapters or

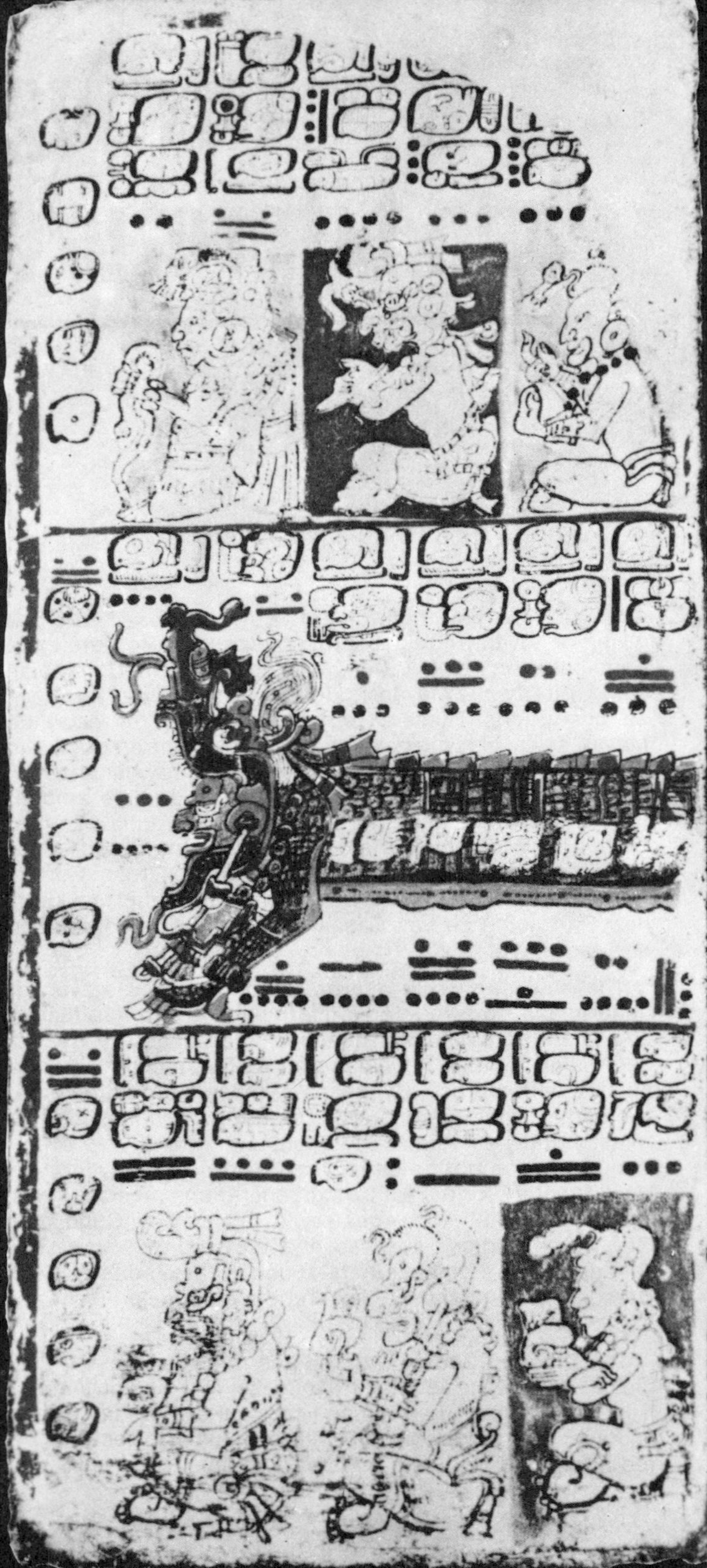

The codices were painted by expert artists.

introduce a change of subject. The glyphs themselves are painted in red, blue, yellow, sepia, black and green. The codex has thirty-nine pages in all, some of which were left blank. The full length of the codex when opened out is 3m 51cm. It came to light in Vienna to where it was taken from Central America half-way through the sixteenth century along with other gifts for Charles I of Spain who was also the Emperor of Germany, the country where the codex finally finished its journey.

The Trocortesian Codex was found in Madrid between 1860 and 1870. The codex had fallen into the hands of two people–Juan de Tro y Ortolano possessed the larger portion and José Ignacio Miró had the rest. It was called the Cortesian Codex because it is believed that Hernán Cortés brought it with him to the royal court. It is now housed in the Spanish capital. The Dresden Codex is a finer example than the Madrid Codex which chiefly describes magic and ceremonies held by the Mayans. Not all the glyphs have been deciphered yet.

A page from the Dresden Codex which is one of three belonging to the Mayan culture.

The Parisian Codex was discoverd wrapped in paper on which was written the name "Pérez" — nothing more. It was unearthed in Paris in 1860 where it had been lying in a basket of rather worthless documents in the National Library. It is incomplete, in poor condition and some parts of it have still to be decoded. Its glyphs, however, are very fine indeed, showing great technique similar to that of the sculptures and basreliefs found in El Naranjo, Piedras Negras and Quiriguá.

Glyphs found on steles, temples, pots and paintings are similar to those of the codices. At Kalakmul, there are no less than one hundred and three steles and thirty of them have completely different markings and glyphs.

Tikal, the largest city in the Mayan world, is equally rich in this sense and there are also many altars and lintels there, the largest and most beautiful of which crowns temple number IV — the Temple of the Great Jaguar. There are also other fine carvings on sapodilla plum wood there. A stele was discovered in Tikal in 1959 (stele 29) on which the date 8-12-14-8-15 (292AD) appears. This is twenty-eight years before the Leyden plate which had been calculated to be the oldest surviving Mayan artifact of the Classic Period.

Apart from numbers, there is a lot yet to be deciphered of the Mayan glyphs. When the key to the Landa "alphabet" was broken there were high hopes of interpreting glyphic texts. These hopes were soon dashed, however, and many of those who have tried to use the so-called "alphabet" have met only with failure. The Mayans had special symbols which they used to denote place names, the names of people, dates and colors. They also had names for the months and their astronomical calculations.

S. Eric Thompson has the following to say on the subject: "Mayan hieroglyphics were sculpted, or more exactly, were carved on stone steles, altars, markers and ball-game (pelota) rings. There are also example found on steps, panels, walls, stone and wooden lintels and on the under surfaces of wooden roofs. Stucco was another material used to form them and they can also be seen engraved on personal items (for example on pieces of jade or shell) and painted on pottery, walls and in books. These hieroglyphics are much, much more complex than those used by the Aztecs.

Extract from a page of the Trocortesian Codex. The National Library of Madrid.

"The Mayans did not possess an alphabet nor a syllabic form of writing except in cases where most of the words are monsyllabic. A form of simple phonetic writing was widely used which we can describe as an advanced form of pictorial writing — at times the pictures were simplified to such an extent that it is difficult to see what they were originally meant to portray.

"Ideographic glyphs were used extensively by the Mayans; for example, the head of the fish, **Xoc**, was difficult to carve and was readily confused with the heads of other animals. In Mayan mythology, there were animals that zoologists have failed to recognise. Consequently, the Mayans often substituted the image of a fish for an ideogram which was the symbol for water. The logic behind this was that the close relation between the fish and the element in which it lives, water, would conjure up an image of **Xoc**. The symbol for water was a jade bead which was arrived at by the fact that both water and jade are green in color and highly valued. Thus, jade suggested water, water suggested **Xoc** who in turn, was seen to equal "beads". As we can see, this system is extremely complex.

"Quite a remarkable feature of Mayan writing is that most of the glyphs and perhaps all of them, have two completely different forms which can be used interchangeably. One is direct, the other, a symbolic or ideographic image generally containing some attribute or element which would remind the reader of the glyph– for example, if we were to draw two keys in the form of a cross instead of writing "Saint Peter." The day known as **Cimi**, or Death, could be carved or painted as the head of the god of death or be represented by a symbol which is similar to our percentage sign — an attribute of that god. In many cases, the symbol figures on the body or the clothing of the god. For the initiated, such a symbol would represent the god of death and would be easily recognised just as the crossed keys would remind a Christian of Saint Peter.

"Almost all glyphs are compounds made up of one principal element to which affixes are added. Prefixes can appear on the left or be incorporated in the main element itself. Suffixes appear on the right or below. The decisive factor in determining where a prefix or suffix ought to go depends on the artistic talents of the "writer". In other words, positioning depended on how the available space could best be filled. Leaving aside the exceptions for the time being however, a prefix could not occupy the place of a suffix or vice versa without altering the meaning of the hieroglyphic compound. The glyph representing "bead" is a good example of a compound. As we said before, the principal element of this glyph is the head of the fish **Xoc**, or the symbol representing water, its counterpart. Afixes

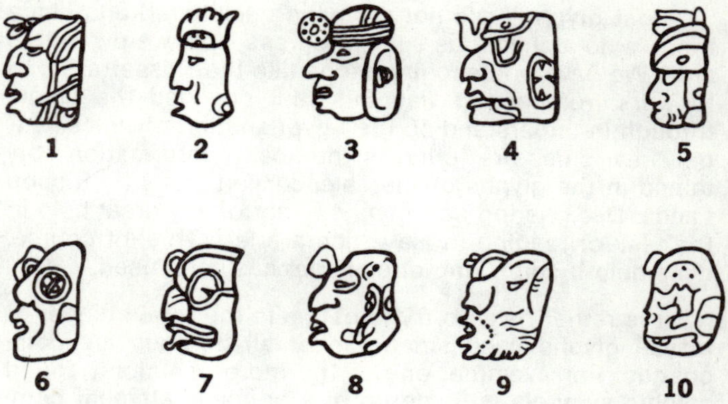

Head numerals from 1 to 10

are prepositions and adverbs which alter the meaning of the glyph. An element which looks like a small torch and which appears as a suffix in all examples of the aforementioned compound, represents the locative preposition "you", "until", "in", or "since". The prefix on the left or above is the symbol for "forwards". The third afix which never appears when the prefix for "forwards" appears is a suffix meaning "backwards". Thus, afixes are used to modify meaning. Our compound therefore, reads as "bead forwards until" and the other, "bead backwards from". Such scope for variation (there are eight possible normal combinations of these elements) does not make reading the glyphs an easy task.

"Until now, already identified afixes include adjectives, adverbs, prepositions and relative pronouns. Mayan writing is nevertheless flexible enough for it to be possible for an afix to change places with the principal element or to become an "infix" within the main element. In other words, the afix may be omitted if its principal feature is added as a detail to the main glyph. In this way, two glyphs can be readily confused as one given the combination of the essential elements of each to form a new glyph.

"The Mayans wrote in simple sentences and I rather doubt if they had afixes to express pronouns and verb tenses. In fact, verbs were very weak in the Mayan language and would be more correctly described as verbal nouns. Bearing this in mind, an example of a sentence found in a divinatory almanac can be tentatively translated as follows: "He influences the corn, the god of death. Death will accumulate among us" or, as we would be more likely to say, "Since the god of death now controls the growth of the corn, many will die.

"Most glyphs have not yet been deciphered and since there is no alphabet as such, progress is very slow in this area. We have no decoding stone like the Rossetta Stone to work from and it was this that provided the breakthrough in understanding the Egyptian hieroglyphics. Our only real clues are found in the scanty information contained in the glyphs of the calendar left to us by Bishop Landa. Deciphering new glyphs is not of any great help in the task of reading those which are left. This, of course, does help if some kind of alphabet has been used.

"It is rather risky to try to estimate the total number of Mayan glyphs used since almost all of them are compounds. For example, one of the more commonly found glyphic symbols is made up of a principal element combined with approximately eighty different arrangements of infixes. Some afixes may be variants of others which, of course, considerably reduces the total number of different meanings. Furthermore, symbolic meanings can also be attributed to afixes as well as them also comprising the principal elements in some cases. The Mayans were not very fond of exact repetitions and so very often sculptors (and writers to a somewhat lesser extent) used all the variations possible of the glyphs to avoid repeating them several times throughout a text. It is certain that many of these variations of known glyphs and those still unrecognised, have still not been identified. Doubts such as these spoil any calculations made to determine the number of glyphs with different meanings.

"In some inscriptions (mainly the compounds for dates and calculations) a great number of the glyphs can be read. On others, however, which deal chiefly with descriptions of rituals and the like, the percentage of the glyphs understood is very low and in some texts, nobody has been able to read any of the glyphs at all.

At the end of the colonial period in Guatemala and Mexico written material comprising chronicles, testimonies, tales, accounts of events etc., was relatively abundant in the areas where the indigenous population had settled. Unfortunately much of this material disappeared due to the state of neglect the libraries were left in after the country gained its independence. On top of this, earthquakes, floods, fires and political urest have cast further shadows on the Mayan literary scene.

When Father Charles Etienne Brasseur de Bourburg from France visited Guatemala, he made many friends there who granted him permission to copy and translate documents as well as to take others back with him to France. He included these documents in the first volume of his book, **"Histoire des Nations Civilisées du Méxique et de**

Mayan glyphs. Most glyphs have yet to be deciphered. Quiriqúa, Guatemala.

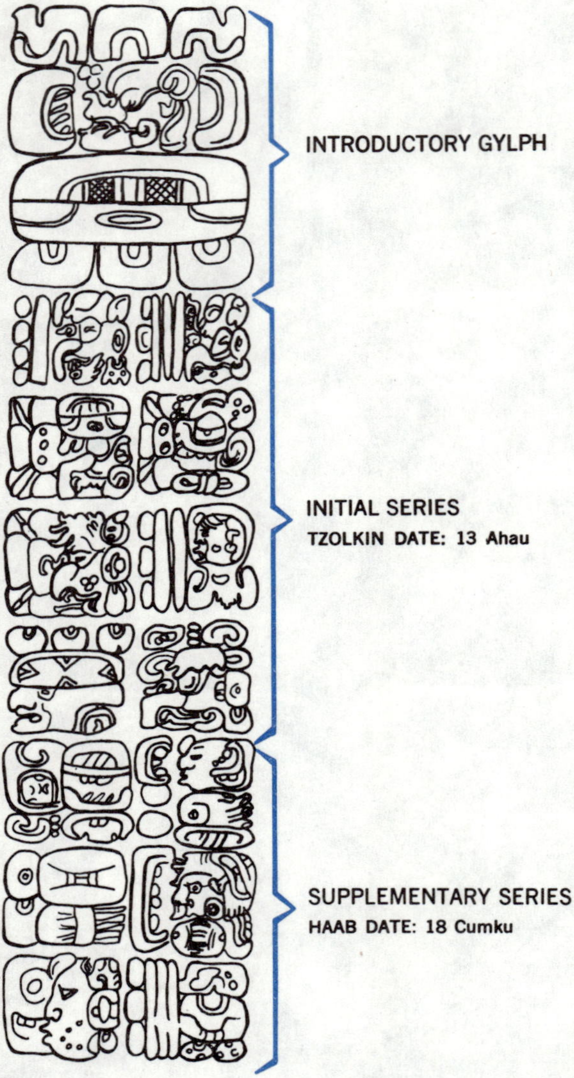

Stele E. de Quiriguá: the introductory glyph, the initial series and the sumplementary series. The date indicated is 9.17.0.0.0 13 Ahau, 8 Cumku which Sylvanus Morley interprets as approximately 771 A.D. This is the largest known Mayan stele, measuring 10.5 in height and weighing about 65 tons.

l'Amérique Centrale durant les siècles antérieures à Christophe Colomb, écrite sur des documents originaux et inédits, puisés aux anciennes archives des indigènes", published in Paris in 1857.

When Father Charles died, his collection of books and papers was split up and some found their way into French and American University libraries.

The Books of **Chilam Balam** chronicles, stories and resumés written in the Yucatán by the Mayans are fairly numerous and provide valuable sources of information. These books are written in Mayan using Latin script and get their name from **chilam** meaning "priest" and **balam** meaning "jaguar". **Balam** also means a secret, esoteric power.

The books contain important material on the times before the Conquest, astronomical tables and provide a great legacy of myths, prophecies, invocations and legends.

The articles comprising the books of the Chilam Balam came from various parts of the Yucatán and in order to distinguish each of them, they were given the names of the places where they were discovered. Thus we have the Chumayel Chilam Balam, the Maní Chilam Balam and the Tizimín Chilam Balam, etc. The most important of the books is the Chumayel Chilam Balam and it came to light during the nineteenth century. The texts of the Chilam Balam were translated into Spanish by Antonio Mediz Bolio in 1930 and were subsequently translated into English in 1933.

From the historical point of view, the most important parts of the Chilam Balam Books are the **u Kablay Katunob** which are compendiums of the **Katunes** (period of twenty years). These were compiled to make a permanent record of the most important events of the time. It is believed that the **u Kablay Katunob** are literal versions of the old codices which were destroyed by the Conquistadores.

Others important articles on the Mayans' spectacular past come from the Uplands of Guatemala.

Pride of place is occupied by the **Popol Vuh** or "Book of Advice" or "Book of the Community" originally written in Quiché. Next in importance are the "annals of the Cakchiqueles" or "The Tecpán Atitlán Biography" and "The title of the Gentlemen of Totonicapán", etc. A play has survived to present times and it is considered to be a unique and most noble gem of literary art. It is called **Rabinal Achí** (The Man From Rabinal) and is written in Quiché. (The annals were written in Cakchiquel).

The Popol Vuh

The **Popol Vuh** is the national book of the Quichés and Guatemala and is also known by the name of the "Chichicastenango Manuscript" after the part of the Quiché region in which it was discovered at the end of the seventeenth century by the Dominican monk, Brother Francisco Ximénez. Brother Francisco translated it into Spanish and as a work of literary art, it ranks amongst the most important. It is invaluable as it includes the principal cosmogenic elements of American prehistory, describing the genesis of the people, floods, their migrations, religion, myths, traditions, the battles they fought and their wisdom.

There we find the records of the Creation, Man's downfall, the eternal battle between good and evil, the search for, and the discovery of the Promised Land (El Quiché) right up until the sad times during which they ceased to be a noble race and were overcome by the Conquistadores.

Equally valuable are the written words left for posterity by the Europeans who recorded the New World as they saw it at that time.

Landa, Cogolludo, Ximénez, Fuentes y Guzmán and Remesal rank among the forerunners of indigenous literature born after the Conquest.

There are numerous "works" in existence such as dictionaries, religious works, word lists, sermons and lectures, catechisms, references to languages, stories and speeches which were written by priests in their eagerness to convert the natives. They have proved to be useful sources of information on customs, the work and interests of the Mayans and the neo-Mayan tribes. The following are but a few examples: "Notebooks on the Cakchiquel Language" by Fray Pedro de Betanzos; "Dictionary of the Tzendal Language", by Fray Domingo de Ara; "Motul Dictionary", by Fray Antonio de Ciudad Real; "Dictionary of Pokomchí Words", by Fray Dionisio de Zúñiga; "Religious Hymns in Quekchi", by Father Luis de Cáncer; "The Art of the Mayan Language", by Fray Juan Coronel; "The Art of the Mayan Language", by Fray Beltrán de Santa Rosa María; "The Art of the Metropolitan Language of the Cakchiquel Kingdom", by Fray Ildefonso José Flores; "Maya-Spanish Dictionary", by Juan Pío Pérez; "The History of the Yucatán" by Lizana, etc.

Other works have disappeared such as: "Sacred and Profane Information on the Antiquities and the Convertion of the Indians"; "The Great Dictionary or Calepino of the Mayan Language"; "Treatise on the Greatness of New Sapin"; "Dictionary of Names, People, Songs, Idols, Dance and

Glyphs from a stone in the Sun Temple, Palenque, Chiapas, Mexico.

other Antiquities from Yucatán"; "A History of the Indians—Their Fables. Superstitions. Customs and Sayings" etc. Books which date up to mid-seventeenth century have survived.

From this we can conclude that before the Conquest, there was an original, autochtonous literature in existence in America which is worthy of close study and more praise. It is very unfortunate indeed that most of it was lost although we can get a glimpse into its greatness and splendor from the literary works left intact.

Mayan literature is boundlessly fantastic and extremely sad. Let us look now at a poem. (This poem was translated into Spanish by Antonio Mediz Bolio.)

Sad, sad star
adorning night's depths

mute with fear in the house of sadness.
The sound of a fearful trumpet rings deafly
in the hall of the noble's home.
The dead do not understand, the living will understand.
Every moon, every year, every day, every breath of wind
continues on its way and passes by too;
thus, all blood reaches its harbour of calm,
just as it reaches its throne and power."

"Red bees spill over the land of the east;
the red rose is their cup; their flower, the red flower.
White bees flood the land of the north;
the white rose is their cup; their flower, the white flower.
Black bees spill over the land of the west;
the black lily is their cup; their flower, the black flower.
Yellow bees flood the land of the south;
the yellow lily is their cup. The yellow flower is their
[flower.

"Singing, I will ring
the harmonious, sonorous instrument.
You, delighted by the flowers,
dance and praise omnipotent God.
Let us enjoy this brief delight
for life is but a fleeting moment."

From the Tizimín Chilam Balam:

"Eat, eat for you have bread;
drink, drink for you have water.
On that day, dust shall overcome the earth,
on that day, a plague will cover the face of the earth,
on that day, a cloud will rise,
on that day, a strong man will seize power in the land,
on that day, homes will tumble in ruins,
on that day, the tender leaf will be destroyed,
on that day, there will be three signs in the tree,
on that day, three generations will hang there,
on that day, the battle flag will be raised
and (men) will scatter far into the woods.

This terrible, prophetic poetry is typical of the poems to be found in the **Chilam Balam** books.

During the Classic Period, (early) Mayan literature was oral, abstract, antiphonal and extensively symbolic. There is little remaining of this literature although there are well-founded beliefs that it was rich, musical, diaphanous, exciting and as mysterious as the Mayan soul tinged with fatality and eternity

Architecture

It is very clear that before the arrival of the Europeans, the concept of a city for the people of Mesoamerica differed considerably from the concept held by the Conquistadores.

"The Mayan civilizations had vast open spaces at their disposal and given their agricultural life-style, they accorded great importance to the rural areas surrounding their settlements since most of their daily activities were of an out-door nature.

"They built cities with the purpose of providing the people with a meeting place for social and political events which were attended during specific times of the year, mainly on feast days when ceremonial rites were carried out. The people also gathered there in times of emergency to receive instructions from their political leaders or priests.

"This explains why the Mayan architects were chiefly influenced by religious precepts and astronomy when planning the cities.

"Cities were composed of a citadel, temples and palaces for worship and for the leaders of the people and the priests to live in. They also had at least one ball-court and other buildings were constructed in blocks around the center of the city. As the population increased, more buildings were added. The houses in which the people lived were grouped around these main buildings and in many instances, were quite far from the center of the city. Little remains today of these houses as they were nearly always made out of perishable building materials. In some cities, the buildings were very cramped together and in others they were built according to the lay of the land.

"In many cities, large courtyards or squares separate the buildings and these served the purpose of providing meeting places. The Mayan architects showed a preference for wide open spaces." (Samayoa Chinchilla.)

In some cases, the citadel was built on a naturally high lying piece of ground. When there were no suitable natural mounds where they wanted to build the city, they created them as they did to reach the famous heights of the great citadel at Tikal.

In early times buildings were made of clay or stucco. Several of these edifices look like truncated pyramids such as can be seen at Uaxactún, Piedras Negras and Zaculeu. Wooden structures were generally erected on top of these elevated platforms and these had straw roofs. The oldest of these mud buildings is the inner pyramid, E-VII-Sub, at Uaxactún.

The use of mud and clay as a building material was surpassed by stone which was used to build temples, palaces and burial chambers.

Thus, architectural art reached its peak during the Classic Period and rivarly existed between the communities of the cities who all tried to out-do each other in varying the architectural style of their city to distinguish it from its neighbor.

To return to the words of Thompson, "Kaminal Juyú (Valley of the Dead) which lies just outside Guatemala City, was one of the major cities of the early Classic Period. Its history dates back well to the limits of the Formative Horizon from which time it continued into the later days of the Classic Period.

"Kaminal Juyú is of particular interest to archaeologists given the rich tombs found within its rather unprepossessing pyramids. The contents of these tombs display a marked influence from Central Mexico and in particular are reminiscent of Teotihuacán. These strange influences are also reflected in some of the pyramids which have horizontal slabs, decorated at the top and bottom with moldings similar to those at Teotihuacán. This influence is not seen in any Mayan city in the lowlands with the exception of Chichén Itzá where there are constructions corresponding to the Mexican period.

"Furthermore, the building materials used in the construction of the pyramids are totally different from those used in the lowland cities.

"None of the stone temples have vaulted roofs — on the contrary holes for posts have been discovered which would indicate that the buildings had roofs of straw. Kaminal Ju-

The pyramid of Cobá, Quintana Roo in Mexico, is surrounded by jungle.

The Castle at Chichén Itzá, Yucatán, Mexico. This was the largest city of the Post-classic period.

yú is also exceptional in that it has an extraordinary number of ball-courts within its urban precincts.

"The cities of El Petén are constructed in limestone and dolomite was commonly used in some parts of the Usumacinta valley. In Copán, Honduras, a very attractive variety of green trachite was used and the Mayans of Quiriguá used sandstone for their buildings and pillars. A crystalline limestone was used in Lubbantún, and on the western boundaries of the Mayan world, in Comalcalco, Tabasco and El Bellote, near Lubaantun, the buildings were made of baked bricks some of which are worked with simpie designs. These are just some of the few places where baked bricks were used.

"In early times at Kaminal Juyú, the pyramids were built of clay. Later they were covered with pumice stone mixed with mud and then with a thin layer of concrete made from fine gravel. Finally, the pyramid was covered with a lime-based layer of plaster."

"Some places are distinguished by the form of their steles. At Cancuén, south of El Petén, for example, steles with crenellated pinnacles were erected making a welcome change from the usual, blunt, rounded-off steles seen in most Mayan settlements.

"Cities vary quite considerably in size from one center to another and this can be attributed to more than just the availability of building material. For example, there are very few steles at Holmul (center-west of El Petén) whereas at Pusilhá (south of Belize) they exist in great abundance. Most of them are small mounds of rock and smooth pebbles without any final layer of plaster to finish them off. Pusilhá is unusual in that it is barely forty-eight kilometers from Lubaantún. From the vessels and figures found there, we can gather that both flourished at around about the same time. There are no steles at all, however, at Lubbantún although there are some very fine examples of masonry.

"Pusilhá was in fact sculpted out of the limestone which was always used for making steles. It is very likely that the monoliths at Pusilhá were not originally just mounds of piled-up smooth pebbles but had been finished with a layer of fine stucco plaster after the gaps between the stones had been filled in with mortar (which has long since crumbled away), to form an even surface for the final coating of stucco."

The temples and palaces are the prototypes of Mayan architecture, the former being a solid rectangular structure in the form of a terraced pyramid. Usually these did not have any doors, windows, or space inside. The exceptions

The Nuns Quadrangle at Uxmal,
Yucatán, Mexico. Below
reconstruction of the building.

Temple number 1 at Tikal, Guatemala.

to this are the pyramids at Uaxactún and Palenque which have tombs inside.

Palaces were divided into chambers with the center of gravity of the upper stories of the structure resting on the outside walls to ensure stability.

Temples and palaces are composed of a substructure, or pyramid base; the main structure; and a suprastructure which, in some cases was built behind the battlements of the building. (There is a classic example of this at Yaxchilán, Chiapas.)

In most cases, the buildings were not decorated beyond the midway point. Decoration was reserved for the upper regions or the façade in the middle of the structure. One exception to this is the sculpted flight of stairs at Copán which is unique in the Mayan world and of unparalleled beauty.

The pyramid was used as the venue for funerals and other ceremonial rites. The architectural impact of the pyramid from any point from which you may choose to view it is truly impressive. The isolation of its bulk, solidity and stability, along with the harmonious symmetry of its lines, its perfect simplicity and lack of decoration, arrouses thoughts of grandeur and majesty.

It is believed that in the old times when an important person died, he was inhumed in a tomb on which stones were piled. These stones were added to periodically as a matter of ritual. Thus, the mass of the tomb increased and in order to keep the small stones together, the gaps were filled in with mortar thus giving birth to the pyramids.

Mayan architects had excellent raw materials at their disposal although they lacked metal tools and animals to do heavy work. They were also ignorant of the wheel and the physical laws of real arches. This all means that they must have taken a long time to complete the "intellectual feat" talked of by Thompson. The problem posed by roofs was solved in Uaxactún first by the use of a system of arches constructed of polished stones projecting from the outside face of the wall. Corbels or false arches were not introduced until the early part of the fourth century AD. These were a Mayan invention, later employed all over the American continent.

Flat roofs were also used and were made of wooden beams and lime cement during the Classic and Post-classic Periods.

The drawback of the false arch is that it cannot be used to provide cover for a large area. Thus, buildings had to be divided into passage-like chambers which, although they were connected by doorways, were damp, narrow and poorly ventilated. It is felt that these were not rooms as such, but were used to store objects needed during acts of worship.

During the Classic Period, the features decorating buildings were rather somber and in the form of friezes, cornices and bases covered with plaster moldings. Later, the Mayans decorated the upper parts of their buildings with stucco. Palenque has some excellent examples of decorations of this type and hieroglyphic inscriptions worked in lime stucco. With the exceptions of Copán and Quiriguá, stone was used for decorative purposes during the Classic Period although it was at this time that the Mayans started to erect sculptures in courtyards and to carve stone panels on walls and ramps next to flights of steps.

This austerity was followed in the Post-classic Period by decorative features of extraordinarily complicated designs.

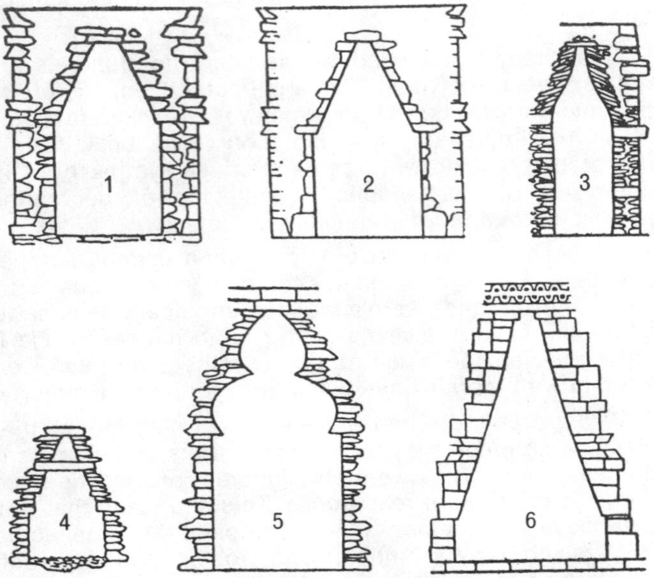
1
2
3
4
5
6

Sayil, Yucatán, Mexico. Detail from the Palace façade.

The Chenes region led this artistic "renaissance" along with the Puuc (both from Mexico) which has been hailed as the "crib of neoclassic architecture distinguished by exuberant, geometric designs, latticework and impressive wall-masks".

From the late Classic Period until the Post-classic Period, "Mayan architecture reached heights unequaled by anyone else in pre-Hispanic América. During this time, motifs multiplied because of the disproportionate and amazing world of fantasy believed in by the Indians of this time. Examples can be seen on masonry, stucco work, mosaics and paintings. Walls, squares, colonnades, ramps, struts, architraves, steps and panels are covered with carvings giving the impression of an a elaborate form of latticework. Such was the new and lavish expression of Mayan art in architecture and it highlighted the loss of the dignity of

Different examples of the Mayan or False Arch.

Archway at the entrance to the Governor's Palace, Uxmal, Yucatán, Mexico.

Burial chamber inside the Temple of Inscriptions. This stone is exquisitely worked with reliefs; Palenque, Chiapas, Mexico.

The walled city of Tulum rises on the shores of the Caribbean in Quintana Roo, Mexico.

The Temple of the Sun; Palenque, Chiapas, Mexico.

sculpting which became a secondary art lacking impetus and grandeur and was solely given to the production of small imperfect images." (Samayoa Chinchilla.)

The two oldest cities are those of Tikal and Uaxcactún. In the northern citadel of Tikal was discovered the oldest known inscription on stele number 29 which is some twenty-eight years before the Leyden plaque (320 AD) and thirty-six years older than stele nine at Uaxactún.

The largest cities of the Mayan world are at Tikal and Copán (Classic Period) and at Chichén Itzá and Uxmal (Postclassic). Chichén Itzá was the most important city of the New Empire and was built by the Itzaés when they migrated from Petén-Itzá during the fourth century. Two styles of art and life alternate gracefully there — old Mayan with Toltec-Mayan. Uxmal, which was built by the Xiues (Mexican Mayans of the tenth century) boasts the most elegant buildings of the Puuc era: the Palace of the Governor; the Nunnery Quadrangle; the Pyramid of the Magician; and, as in Chichén Itzá, there are temples to Kukulcán (Gucumatz in Maya-Quiché, Quetzalcóatl in Náhuatl) and to the warriors. These four great cities deliver the mystical message left by the Mayans for the rest of mankind.

Sculpture combined with architecture.
Masks from Kohunlich, Quintana Roo, Mexico.

Sculpture

The origins of sculpting as an art form in the Mayan world probably began much as they did in other parts of Mesoamerica. The earliest lintels, altars and pillars were made from wood. However, it is very probable that a great number of wooden artifacts have been lost given the destructive effects of damp and microfauna on this material. In this way, we may have lost records of the first studies of time and the beginnings of hieroglyphic writing. Later, clay figures were fashioned by hand. These were nearly always of human beings either naked or half dressed with slanting eyes, their heads out of proportion in relation to the size of the rest of the body.

Turbans, crests, necklaces and chokers were made by rolling small balls of clay into the desired form of each separate component. These components were assembled before the items were finally baked.

Figures carved from stone blocks date from the beginning of the fourth century A.D. and the earliest of these show a lesser degree of beauty than those made from clay or wood. Eyes, noses and mouths are often nothing more than simple incissions in the face and in many cases the upper and lower limbs are crossed as this made the task of the sculptor easier. Often, the figure's elbows rest on its knees.

The tools of the sculptor were chisels made of basalt or obsidian, silex or obsidian (**chay**) knives, bone awls and

Stele B from Copan in Honduras is a magnificent example of Mayan sculpture.

Reconstruction of stele B, Copan. In this, we can appreciate more fully its detailed work. The crests in the upper section look remarkably like elephant heads.

A woman carrying a child on her back. From the Island of Jaina, Campeche, Mexico. Pieces of great artistic quality were worked in Jaina.

A highrelief from stele 1 in Bonampak, Chiapas, Mexico.

mallets made of flint or wood. Collections have been made of tools made of obsidian. Fine needles and pins, knives and chisels were uncovered and have proved to be particularly fine examples of craftmanship, capturing the essence of effort, given that they are often worked and shaped on all sides.

Soft limestone which is easily broken away from quarry walls is available in abundance in the area from El Petén to the Yucatán. This meant that the craftsmen were able to work with relatively soft blocks of stone which had not yet been hardened by the elements.

Blocks were removed from the geographical stratum exposed in the walls of the quarries and were worked carefully with crude mallets or chisels. Another more complicated method used to shape the stone blocks involved inserting short needles along the desired edge. Then the blocks were heated over resin fires after which cold water was poured into the holes left by the needles to split the rock in that direction.

Rollers, levers and strong ropes made of sisal or hemp were used to transport the block to the eventual site of the monument. This task naturally demanded enormous effort and the pushing of many strong arms to move the rock to the hole that was dug to stand the rough block of mineral in.

Pillars and columns originated in this fashion and the carving of religious motifs on these monoliths marked the half-way point in the task. The first step in the process of decoration was to carve the hieroglyphics. After this had been completed, other artists took over to sculpt and carve designs before handing over to the painters who finished off the task which had been so painstakingly undertaken. When all this was completed, the finished piece was sanded down. Nowadays, we can but marvel at the Mayans' amazing skill in removing lumps of flint from the andesite blocks with their mallets and chisels. The stone that was removed did not go to waste and was used to make mounds. In some cases, they would embed other stones in

This clay model depicting a prisoner with his hands bound was discovered in the highlands of Chiapas, Mexico.

the cavities left by the flint. Stele D at Copán is a prime example of this type of work.

The Mayans decorated ceremonial chambers, rooms, castellations, panels, squares, colonnades, lintels and even the steps of outside terraces (a typical example of this can be seen at Copán, and at Yaxchilán there are decorated castellations).

Sculptures and monoliths were erected in squares and courtyards as well as at the entrances of temples and palaces. Steles carved with dates and events both happy and sad have also been found in these places. The collection of monuments surrounding the great temples of Tikal is especially fine.

The oldest example of Mayan sculpture in stone is at the ceremonial center in Uaxactún which was worked in the fourth century BC. Stele number nine is outstanding. It is uneven in size and the designs carved on it are stylistically rigid in relation to their anatomical proportions although they show original style like that of the new esthetic trends. Figures of men appear with their heads facing us and their arms and legs in profile. This position was abandoned during the following century.

Style evolved in the next century and man was depicted face-on. This trend was possibly developed in Uaxactún and the oldest surviving example was discovered there — stele 26 which dates from the year 445 AD. Another example of the new artistic trend is the figure on stele 4 at Tikal the arms, head and body of which all face forwards. The new style was copied in Toniná, Piedras Negras, Palenque, Quiriguá and later in Copán. In Piedras Negras, people were sculpted face-on and seated in vaulted niches with their legs crossed.

Stone sculpture continued in this fashion until the Mayan Golden Age when it positively flourished in a way unrivalled throughout the rest of the continent. Over a period of four hundred years, Mayan artists acquired considerable mastery over their skills.

"The decisive impulses in art continued to be repeated symbolism, hieratic attitudes and the subjegation of esthetic expression to the secret demands of the soul which lent the figures an air of serenity, enigma and inner strength.

"Despite the restrictions imposed by theocracy and custom, sculpted forms which were the product of a combination of artistic skills and diligence developed during a time of restrictions.

"Lines became softer and purer and proportions were balanced — in short, there was a marked shift towards abandoning static poses in favor of being truer to life and basking in its sources. Unmistakable indications of spontaneity, disquiet and other surprising aspects all seeking new directions in which to realize the desires of the people are to be found all over the Mayan world.

"Rough lumps of stone awoke from centuries of slumber to take on the forms of gods and men, animals and plants. A third dimension, depth, was added to those already known and this increased the feeling of reality surrounding the figures. A pleasant consequence of the liberating fervor implied by such progress is the fact that the sculptures and bas-reliefs of this age are fine examples of solid, polished plastic thought.

"The ancestral disciplines are still respected although through their persistence which is, without a doubt, due to the mystical and traditional feelings of the people, each Mayan city strove to distinguish itself by adding personal touches which later proved to be very useful in identifying the work produced by the various Mayan tribes. These differences, however, relate purely to form and they did not alter the basic layout or style of the cities. The reliefs depicting human figures at Copán and Quiriguá are overwhelmed by symbolic motifs. The people of these cities did not suddenly change to follow the realistic style of Palenque or the burgeoning dynamism of Piedras Negras or Yaxchilán, preferring to stick proudly to their old esthetic ideals and their complacent interpretation of the Universe." (Samayoa Chinchilla.)

Approximately four hundred examples of large sculptures from the times of the Classic Period have been discovered and there must be many thousands more buried away in the jungle. Well over a thousand smaller pieces of sculpture have been recovered.

Steles 12 and 14 at Piedras Negras are particularly fine pieces of work and are prime examples of "the austere grandeur of artistic works since Mayan artistic sentiment was not exclusively expressed in hieroglyphics." Morley finds stele 12 extraordinary and feels that its different planes are an essay in the art of perspective. Stele 14 is alluringly beautiful and perfect in its finish.

To continue with our inventory of the eternal, lintel 3 at Piedras Negras shows a **Halach Uinic** (real man) receiving his vassals while seated on a throne. The panel on the Sun Temple at Palenque depicts two priests making offerings before a ceremonial shield on which the face of the star king appears.

The lintels of building 23 at Yaxchilán; the head of an ocelot and steles A, D, M, and N at Copán; monolith E at Quiriguá which is the largest sculpture crafted by the Mayans; stele F and the animal altars O and P, also at Quiriguá are all remarkable too.

These pieces capture the elegance of the movement and the bewitching magic which impells the spirit to express itself in art. To continue with our list, the following are worthy of mention as examples of animal sculpture and imagery; the masks on the walls of the Magician's house at Uxmal, the strange stuccos on the Convent, the motifs on throne 1 at Piedras Negras, and the façade of one of the temples in the great square at Hochob, Campeche (Chenes).

Mesoamerican sculpture is symbolic and esoteric; gods take on the form of human beings and sometimes the forms of animals. Examples are to be found of zoomorphic, phytomorphic and supernatural figures. The disembodied god of death associated with the snake is a compulsory theme in this form of art which is "unemotional but vigorous and transcendental at the same time."

The plastic arts declined with the fall of the Classic Period, indicating that the spirit was losing its vitality.

Chac Mool from Chichén Itzá, Yucatán, Mexico. It is believed that Chac Mool was the messanger of the gods.

Stucco head from Palenque, Chiapas, Mexico. National Museum of Anthropology, Mexico City.

The sculpture of this period was excessively decorative and was limited to adorning the fronts of buildings. As "an art of the independent spirit," sculpture disappeared. The Mayans stopped erecting steles as if it were no longer important to record their fortunes and misfortunes for the sake of posterity. In the Yucatán, reclining figures such as the **Chac Mool**, thrones, standard bearers and the upright Atlantes (Toltec influence) were preferred.

During the Post-classic Period, sculpture was reborn and occupied a place of secondary importance in the grandiose architecture of that time.

Stone disc engraved with a jaguar and ceremonial glyphs. From Chincultic, Chiapas. National Museum of Anthropology, Mexico City.

Stucco sculptures were widely used for decorating the insides and outsides of buildings during the Classic Period and the decorative panels at Palenque and comalcalco are very impressive. Few stucco sculptures were made during the Post-classic Period although examples can be seen at Izamal, Nocuchich, and Acanceh. They are not as fine as those at Palenque, however.

Modelling in clay was a noble exercise for the early Mayans and crude primitive examples were found at Uaxactún. The eyes of the figures are simple holes and their other features are very basic (first and second centuries BC). Later, the lines became more fluid and the expressions acquired a more natural look.

Clay modelling was developed in Jonuta, the island of Jaina, among the people living along the banks of the river Chixoy, the communities at Piedras Negras, Altar de Sacrificios and Mayapán. Later this form of art became rather precocious.

Clay was followed by wood as a favored medium and in turn, was substituted by stone and stucco.

Igneous rock, obsidian and jade were used to make steles and figures at Kaminal Juyú, Santa Lucía Cotzumalguapa and Zaculeu and metamorphic rock, such as the marble of the vessels found at Ulúa (Honduras) was also used as was sedimentary rock (eg. limestone). The altars and steles at El Petén and in the Yucatán are made of limestone. Sandstone was favored at Quiriqúa, andesite in Copán and small pieces of flint in El Petén.

The wealth of expression that could be achieved from working in terracota and the relative ease of modelling this medium are the reasons for the abundance of figures and items made of this material. Some small master-pieces have been uncovered, giving us an insight into daily life, hopes and desires of the people, their suffering and times, of joy as well as other aspects of life which are not illustrated on the monuments. Everything is there right from the gods and men to **totems** and domestic animals, the games of the children and the adult Mayans and even lesser monsters which are often deformed, threatening or wounded and in pain. These hand-crafted figurines date from the Formative Horizon and the molded figures, from the late Classic Period.

On the larger sculptures, man is shown in ritual, hieretic and symbolic attitudes. On the whole, the people on the steles are over-weight with hooked noses, a classic profile and small mouths with generous lips turned down at the corners. They have small molded chins, broad foreheads, large almonds-shaped eyes and long hair often in very elaborate styles and cuts. Their hands and feet which are excellent for communicating expression in Mayan art, are small.

There are few reclining or seated figures among the larger sculptures. Standing figures and those in profile are typical of the Classic Period. In Tikal, the faces look forwards and this trend spread to Quriguá and Copán. After a while, seated figures looking forwards were crafted in Piedras Negras. Later, combinations of front-facing, seated figures and others standing in profile were used in bas-reliefs and high-reliefs.

At the close of the Classic Period (731 AD) the new trend spread and conventional, ceremonial, geometric, decorative and realistic signs were perfected. Amidst a profusion of anthropological, zoomorphological and phytomorphical elements in which snakes, quetzal feathers and maize leaves woven into different shapes predominate, the beauty of the Mayan as the chief figure stands out. These colored forms are a real feast for the eye.

The colors used by the Mayans for painting their images were tones of red, blue, golden yellow, sepia, ochre and green.

Vase showing a dancer dressed in a jaguar skin. From Altar de Sacrificios. Housed in the Aurora Museum, Guatemala City.

Ceramics

In classifying the pieces of ceramics uncovered, we can learn a great deal about the evolution of Mayan culture as well as the dates which relate to each period. The beauty and originality of the pieces are of course indicative of the esthetic levels reached.

All ceramic objects are important in the study of a civilization — right from humble household utensils to the more elaborate items used in religious ceremonies and ornaments which testify the skill of the craftsman.

The following techniques were employed generally to fashion objects from clay and other soft, maleable materials: modeling from a lump or block of material; constructing the object from strips or rolls of material; molding.

The first technique is one of the oldest in the world and is still used to this day by the Indians of the New World. The second method involved making small balls of clay which were then stuck onto the surface of the object by hand for decorational purposes. The third system, molding, has also been in use since ancient times and is used to produce items in large numbers, for example, articles for every-day use. Molds were used to either make a whole object or just part of an object.

In general, the ancient Mayans did not fire their pottery in ovens but left the articles to harden outside in the open air. This is a very primitive method. The results, however, compare favorably with the finest artifacts to be found anywhere in the world.

The Mayans excelled in the ceramic arts and their settlements are full of pieces and fragments which, when classified into periods or phases, provide us with an exact scale for determining the development of their culture through its genesis, zenith and downfall.

In El Petén, Chiapas, and the highlands and lowlands of the Mayan world, pieces of baked clay, jars, ampullas, earthenware bowls, pots, vessels, idols, figures, whistles, rattles, beads, urns, four-legged pots and other containers in the form of animals, humans and plants, have been uncovered in vast numbers.

The variety of shapes and styles is enormous and includes the discovery of pieces such as bits of drainage pipes, weights for fish hooks, talismans (**alxiks**), spindles and even sections of tiled and concrete covered roads.

Cups, plates and incense burners are often decorated with figures of humans and mythical animals either painted or etched on the surface of the article. High-reliefs of perfect lines were another decorational technique and we can only but admire and enjoy the results produced by these ancient craftsmen.

The facial characteristics on the figures on cups and incense burners fall into different categories: the man of the Classic Mayan Period was beardless or bearded; the second category is determined by the portrayal of the children's faces which had high cheekbones; thirdly, the people depicted look very like what the anthropologists refer to as "Cambodian Man".

Studies carried-out at Uaxactún which is perhaps the oldest Mayan city, have enabled us to establish the major areas of origin. Influence, progress and abandoning of the types of pottery that predominated during the Classic Period (in El Petén) have led us to the conclusion that there was a high degree of uniformity in the development of the ceramic arts all through Mayan culture and neo-Mayan culture.

The periods or phases which correspond to these types are as follows: **Mammón** (grandmother), **Chicanel** (the gobetweens), **Tzakol** (builders) and **Tepeu** (Conquistadores). These names are all taken from the **Popol Vuh**. The fifth phase is known as the Mexican phase.

MAMMON: Pre-classic or Formative Phase, 600 BC-300 AD. Fragments are usually located in the lower stratum of the earth, in what is called "the black earth". They are older than the first works in masonry and even older than the carved, stone steles. Designs on pottery from this phase are monochromatic. Numerous examples have been found in Kaminal-Juyú, Uaxactún, and Totonicapán; the high plains of Chiapas and in Belize. These are simple and rudimentary, made of grey or red clay with etchings on the surface, grooves or modelled motifs. The figures are normally female and their eyes are simple holes made with an awl. Simple round cups with wide lips have been found along with earthenware bowls, plaques and plates.

CHICANEL: Early Classic Age, 300 to 500 AD. Developments in technique are noticable. The pieces are multicolored and are less rigid and uniform in shape. These decorations appear on the contours of cups which are almost always cylindrical. Designs are out-lined in black and are of men, snakes, jaguars, red coati and flowers which were all common later. These objects are found in the strata under the steles. During this phase, caustic acid replaced volcanic ash for engraving. Many examples have been found at Kaminal-Juyú in Guatemala as well as in Acanceh, Mani, Kabah and other sites in the Yucatán peninsula.

TZACOL: Middle Classic Age, 500 to 700 AD. Technical progress noticeable. Geometric designs are painted, modelled, engraved or etched on. The multicolored, clear motifs are of very great beauty and elegance. Backgrounds are usually yellow or orange. This phase is characterized by the introduction of boxes with a border around the base. Large pitchers and drinking vessels with no glaze on the outside surface have been found and in many instances these are decorated with cameos engraved on a defined background to make the motifs stand out clearly.

TEPEU: Late Classic Age, 700 to 900 AD. This period was the zenith of the ceramic arts and crafts. Cups and other vessels show figures painted or worked with great skill on the surface of the pieces. Generally, they are decorated with white, red, black and yellow pigments. The scenes illustrated are very realistic and are historic or religious in theme. Scenes from daily life were also common. The borders and edges of the articles are worked with glyphs which provide dates relating to the scenes depicted and in themselves, are decorative.

During the Late Classic Period, an exceptional type of ceramics appeared called "leaden" pottery. This type was used extensively on the south coast of Guatemala and the coast of Chiapas. Some examples are decorated with designs not generally associated with the Mayans which leads us to conclude that the Mayans did not produce these pieces. By 1200 AD, the Mayans had exhausted their ideas. This leaden pottery is characterized by a brilliant finish which is hard and almost glass-like. It is believed to have been produced by submerging the items in a solution containing iron and aluminium.

The "fine orange" ceramics are also from the Late Classic Period (Puuc phase) and consistently fine examples were found in Teotihuacán and Monte Albán in Mexico and in Kaminal-Juyú, in Guatemala. It was produced in the uplands of Mexico and in many other places.

The use of molds is particular to Late Classic work. There are considerable similarities between the pieces

Urn showing the rolled tablet technique.
Museum of Villahermosa, Tabasco, Mexico.

found at Teotihuacán and in Guatemala. The Classic and Post-classic periods correspond to the production in bulk of incense burners of which a great number have been found in Guatemala and Mexico.

The following are the finest pieces which have been uncovered belonging to the **Tepeu** phase which has neither been equalled nor surpassed: the cup found in structure A 1 at Uaxactún; the plate with the stylized figure of a dancer which came from the same tomb; the cup from one of the valleys of the river Chixoy; the Nebaj cup (El Quiché); the cup from Altar de Sacrificios (from the Guatemalan side of the Usumacinta river) — without a doubt, these pieces are those most representative of the period around 800 A.D.

THE MEXICAN PERIOD: Post-classic, 900 to 1450 AD. This phase corresponds to the abandoning of the larger centers in El Petén. Thus, the focus on ceramics changed and moved to the Yucatán where it flouished, recharged with new ideas regarding decorative techniques which really took ornamentation to excess as did architecture at this time.

Despite the wealth of ornamentation, the Mayans of this age failed to surpass or even match the tasteful, austere elegance of the Middle and Late Classic Periods. Remains of the most recent ancient Mayan pottery are generally multicolored and are often decorated with red designs on a cream or red colored backgrounds. Black motifs on a cream colored background have been found in Mixco Viejo (the Guatemala home of the Pokomam culture). A great number of incense burners decorated with motifs applied to the outside of the vessel have been found dating from this period. The style of these burners is still used by the Lacandon Indians today in Chiapas.

Modeled pottery from the prime of the Classic Period was of poor quality, technically speaking. In the last phases of this period, ceramics provide a real wealth of decoration and finishing methods. Towards the end, esthetic values took priority over durability and utility, and objects with shining surfaces and lively colors were produced.

Thus, the decorative techniques used by the Mayans over the years to give their work an air of distinction include: molding; stippling; openwork; scrapping; modeling; application of bits of clay; and perforation. All these techniques were executed drawing on both the impulses of humor and fantasy. In some instances, the pieces appear simple and often child-like with simple geometric motifs. In others, and in particular in cases where the modeled or painted figures assume attitudes of hierarchy, tragedy, savageness or humor, the results are of an exotic, remote world in which, "men tortured their imaginations constantly in a feverish search for new and surprising creations."

Part of one of the Bonampak murals, Chiapas. The headdresses of the people represent aquatic fauna. Copy in the National Museum of Anthropology, Mexico City.

Painting

Cave painting is one of the most ancient expressions of art known to us left by our forefathers. Examples of this unique, original art form are found in temples, palaces, pyramids and tombs. It is generally believed that buildings such as these were originally covered in paintings, but time and atmospheric conditions have taken their toll on much of Mayan man's esthetic efforts.

Among what remains are the remnants of a mural on a wall of structure B-XIII in Uaxactún which was built in the seventh century A.D. There is a copy of this mural in the Classic Mayan Room at the Museum of Anthropology and Ethnology in Guatemala.

The murals at Bonampak (700 A.D.) were uncovered in 1946 but un-fortunately have also fallen prey to the passing of time and exposure to adverse weather conditions.

Experts have come to the conclusion that the practice of painting murals in Central America dates from the Preclassic Horizon and the remains of paintings have been discovered at Cuicuilco, Cholula, Monte Albán and Mitla in Mexico. (These were not painted by Mayan artists.) Mayan paintings include those at Chichén Itzá, Tulum, Palenque, Corozal, Santa Rita, Tikal, Yaxchilán and other sites. The subjects of these paintings are anthropomorphic and zoomorphic figures, decorative motifs on staggered borders, fluted fillets and monochrome fascias on flat and curved surfaces, fillets, borders and cornices of walls and altars.

This unmistakable style of painting flourished during the dawning of the Classic Period and its characteristics are unique and original. The Mayan artists of this time dispensed with superfluous details, leaving the principal elements to stand out clearly. The forms lack scientific perspective. Outlines for designs were done with red and

Prisoners of war awaiting their fate. From the Bonampak murals, Chiapas. Copy in the National Museum of Anthropology, Mexico City.

black pigments and they used a whole range of colors to paint their expressions of fantasy and Mayan passion.

When talking about pictorial art forms, the paintings on pottery and codices are counted along with the examples already mentioned, and particularly fine examples of pottery painting are found on the cups discovered at Uaxactún, Chamá, Piedras Negras and other sities. The opinion that the techniques of Mayan painting developed alongside those used in sculpting and carving is based on these discoveries. Bowing to religious dictates, the figures are usually painted in a style which deliberately deforms both human beings and objects — "exagerated lines and depictions of mythical fantasies dominated by symbolism lend a feeling of the unnatural to life."

Right from the earliest times, inspiration was of a tribal and religious nature and Mayan artists remained faithful to it through the ages. This symbolic art is difficult to under-

stand in modern times given the prejudices and influences of our westernized culture.

When a Mayan was representing a divine being for example, he paid little regard to the form of the body. Instead, he would emphasise attributes and emblems (of supernatural powers) which, according to his beliefs, were assembled in the superhuman being. Pictures of this type are charged with elements of which symbolism is of the utmost importance — astronomic signs; richly-colored, plumed headdresses; ritual masks; the snake; leaves and cornflowers, and glyphs along the bottom lend balance to the main part of the picture.

Demi-gods and gods prevail in the codices in which the drawings tend to mock form in favor of symbols. The features of esoteric and ritual science were adhered to.

Paul Westheim comments "Nothing is told and nothing is explained. They represented what everybody was familiar with. Meaning is what matters, not the form of the phenomena. The artist appeals to memory and evokes fantastic images to conjure up a great, tremendous and monstrous event or something that could happen if the gods so desired. In other words, the painting is a creation of the imagination, the aim of which is to stimulate religious ideas. Reality as such is not reproduced, but a reality of magical thought is created. It is not enough to appreciate the magic thoughts of the artist — one must interpret his vision in order to discover the hidden mythical meaning of the phenomena. Appeals were made to a suitable means of expression to transform the spiritual into a visible presence and to sustain inner spiritual qualities in the transformation.

"Art's purpose in painting is the same as in the creation of reliefs. That is, the figurative symbols of the codices which are brought together by an inspired, complex and unique system, transform metaphysical concepts into a visibly understandable phenomenon without divesting them of their sacred, mystical character.

"Mural paintings are not miniature images as in the codices, nor are they images of speculative meditation — they provide a clearer language which is more immediate and concise albeit an interpretation of Man's creation and of what Man ought to create."

To make up for any lack of information provided by the codices and murals, there are rewards to be found in pottery. Archaelogists have uncovered many examples of this art form which provide us with illustrations of figures and because the potter often disregarded the conventional forms of deliberate disproportion of figures in establishing a hierarchy of divinities, static poses and monotony were used to the detriment of capturing unexpected, emotive qualities.

For the Mayan painter, the human being was the most important subject and we see people depicted on murals, codices and on cups and vases. The importance of man was not his physical being but his symbolic qualities and the solemnity that the presence of the gods who were embodied in men lent to great ceremonies and liturgies.

"Despite the fact that at first sight some human representations of Mayan art appear too fantastic and unrealistic, there is no doubt that their art is on a par with the work of the Assyrian, Babylonian, Egyptian and Cretian painters who worked in similar styles".

Gods, priests and warriors are very often seen on walls, in reliefs and on cups with penetrating eyes and their faces lit by smiles reminiscent of the looks of a mask. Often they are receiving homage from vassals, holding a ceremonial staff or sceptre while hearing the entreaties of war prisoners wishing to escape death.

The amazing skill of the artists at Bonampak, Chichén Itzá (Temple of the Warriors) and Tulum, captures the essence of the realistic qualities of men, pumas, owls, plumed serpents, apes, tapirs and various birds. Their skill can also be appreciated in the designs on borders, rosettes and of flowers used to decorate public squares. Many examples of skillful painting are seen on moldings, flat moldings, altars and cornices. To achieve such wonderful results, the rules of perspective and the depth of character were ignored in spite of the inborn esthetic instincts which inspired the artists — they never progressed beyond representing their subjects in one dimension.

There are very few murals dating from the Classic Period, the one at Uaxactún was painted in grey, red, yellow and orange on a white background with outlines in black. This mural measures 3 m × 1.25m and shows many figures confined in two areas divided by a horizontal line. On the upper right section, there are two people separated by a column of glyphs who appear to be holding a conversation. On the other side of another column of glyphs, there are more people talking to each other. These murals, however, have been badly damaged by the extreme humidity of the jungle of El Petén.

Down below the dividing line, there are pictures of more people. One is dressed in scarlet and another is in black the two are also separated by a column of glyphs. There is a small temple with a great cornice next to them. There are three people sitting under its roof, dressed in tunics and they appear to be women. Glyphs are painted above the heads of each. To the left, are two figures who look as if

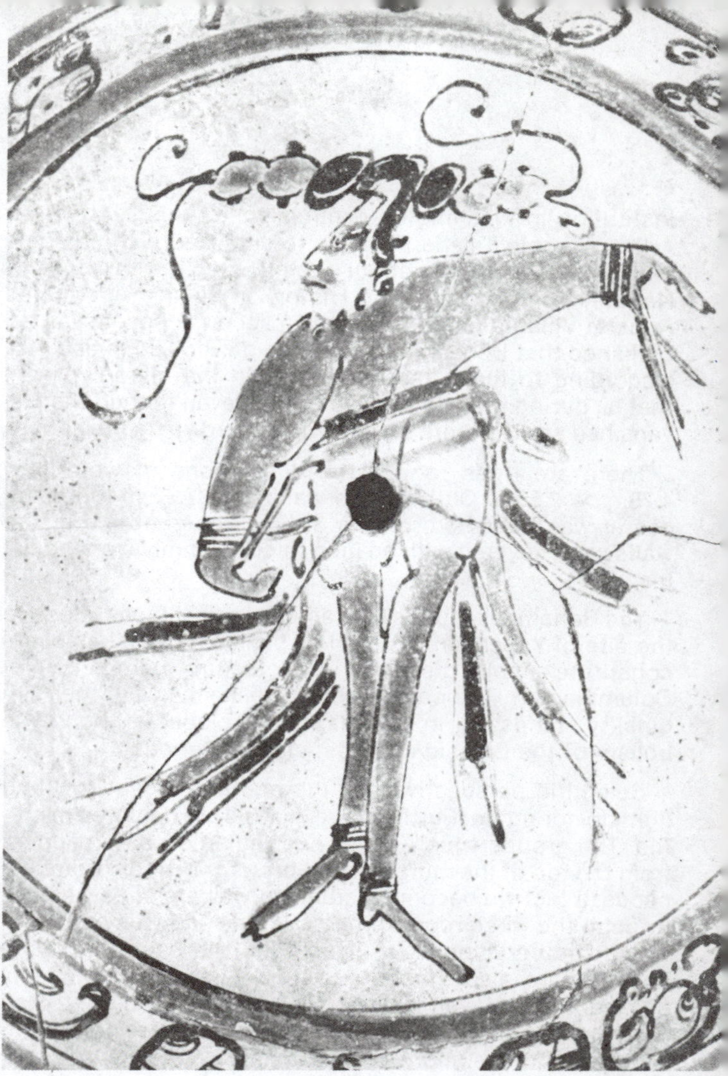

The decoration on a vase from Uaxactún, Guatemala. The dexterity of Mayan artists can also be appreciated in their ceramic art.

they are reading an inscription and seated behind them on the floor is a musician with a drum. Twelve men on their way to the temple are close by him.

The people in this mural appear to be wearing turbans and plumes of feathers. Their clothes are very sumptuous and they are wearing bracelets, necklaces and nose rings. Some are carrying pouches of **pom** (copal resin), weapons, staffs and musical instruments. Below the second area of the mural there is a border with 72 symbols of the day, starting with twelve **Imix** and terminating in 5 **Eb**.

The murals at Bonampak are exquisite examples of artistic talent. After the discovery of the paintings, the Carnegie

Institution in Washington commissioned the Guatemalan Artist, Antonio Tejeda Fonseca to copy and provide some technical information about them. Later the Institute of National Anthropology and History in Mexico contracted Agustín Villagra Calletti to make a second copy. It was established that Bonampak flourished during 600 to 850 A.D. (according to the dates mentioned in the hieroglyphics), that is, during the late Classic Period, even though the Mayans had settled there some two hundred years previously.

There are three rooms, the dimensions of which are 4.75m × 2.50m. Outside, the walls are 27.75 m high. The center was built from blocks of limestone and the inside walls were covered with an inch thick (23 mm) layer of plaster.

The Bonampak murals (Bonampak is in Chiapas, close to the site of Yaxchilán, on the left bank of the Usumacinta) constitute a major discovery in our century as regards pre-Columbian art. Their astonishing lifelikeness and their originality stands out in contrast to the closed artistic symbolism of the Classic and Post-classic Periods.

Scientific perspective and the contrast of shadow and light do not figure. Furthermore, people are depicted in profile. The groups which are wonderfully distributed appear from the top of the murals to the bottom. They are homogeneous, a fact we become increasingly aware of as we pass through the three rooms. The paintings show us battles in which the ceremonies of dance and the sacrifice of the defeated are also illustrated. As we would like to sadly point out, the Mayan tribes often turned on their defeated brothers and sacrificed them. The Mayans were heroic, virtuous, perfidious and weak "reamen."

Paul Westheim feels that "the most significant work of the Bonampak artists found in the murals of the central chamber show scenes of battles, triumph and the sacrifice of the prisoners." These war scenes rank amongst the greatest and most fascinating ever painted.

"We see the warriors in their showy apparel, wearing jaguar skins and great yellow plumes on their heads. They are attacking the enemy (also Mayan with lances, and are cutting locks of hair off their prisoner. The scene is a swarm of tangled figures conveying movement and excitement — a chaos of bodies, masses and color. Each figure and gesture is splendidly captured and portrayed with an epic display of skill. The artist never lost sight of the great unity and structural articulation of the whole scene. He made conscientious use in the organization of the scene of the means of pictorial expression, that is, of color distribution and contrast and the values of a vast flat surface.

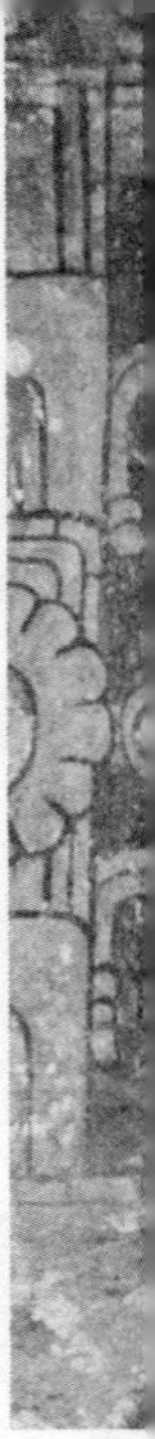

Part of a painting from the Temple of the Friezes, Tulum, Quintana Roo, Mexico.

His lines vibrate and ring with vigor and his staggered use of color is penetrating and strong.

"He captures movement in the violent clash of bodies, revealing the confidence he felt of being in perfect control of the task. To attain this corpreity the artist used color well by blending it. Foreshortenings and intersections are only visible if we look closely.

"The faces of the warriors burn with the excitement of battle. Those who are being defeated and will be sacrificed display pain and resignation to their fate. These facial expressions also speak to us, although not through the conventional convolutions of speech — the leaders are arguing and warriors are singing even though there is no audible evidence of this in the murals. This is yet another proof of the reality of this work and not that of imagination."

The hands are very expressive and the eyes speak — we see haughty pride and hatred; the tribulations, stoicism and tranquility of those doomed to be sacrificed; we feel the pity for those fallen in battle expressed by their brothers who will eventually suffer a similar fate. The vast use of color ranging from brilliant blues in the background to vibrant greens in the plumes worn by the victors is marvelous.

There are more murals dating from the Post-classic Period and these are in better condition than those of the Classic Period. Examples can be seen at Chichén Itzá, and Tulum in Mexico, Santa Rita and Corozal in Belize.

In Chichén Itzá in the Temple of the Warriors and the Temple of the Jaguars, there are two murals of scenes of human sacrifice. One has a sea theme, depicting a coastal village and oarsmen and fishermen in three boats off the shore. The sea is carved with fish, crustacians, molluscs and chelonia. Huts are visible along the coast. We can also see the village people going about their daily tasks — vendors carrying large bundles on their backs, a woman tending a fire and another washing clothes. In the upper right-hand section, there is a small temple with a large mythical snake rising out of it.

Another mural at Chichén Itzá portrays an attack on a village. The terror and violence of the scene is the most notable feature. A totemic serpent rises in a spiral behind one of the invaders, protecting the people and challenging their foe. The people of the village are armed with arrows and lances, fighting frenetically. Higher up and farther off, the women are crying with their arms outstretched at the sight of the bloodied lances. The rhythm of the picture descends from the vertex of the last building to the base of the mural where a couple of fighters struggle in pain.

There is another war mural in the Temple of the Warriors showing prisoners on their way to the consumation of their tragic fate and groups of men fiercely defending the entrance to the sanctuary.

Other murals of the Post-classic Period are religious in theme and examples were discovered at Uxmal, Tulum, Santa Rita and Corozal, symbolic elements were which important during the Classic Period occupied a secondary position during this phase.

Sophisticated techniques, awareness of space, colors and brush strokes are observed in the vignettes of gods, men and animals found in the books of hieroglyphics (particularly in the Dresden Codex). This was a school of art in which artistic canons and secret formulas were upheld with the same ferocity with which their religious and esoteric principles were preserved.

The most important paintings on clay are found on the multicolored cups dating from the Great Age, discovered in Uaxactún and Tikal. Others have also been found in Tabasco and Chiapas.

The cups are original and beautiful in design. Those on which the designs are taken from nature are very true to life and belong equally to real life and the world of mythology.

Jade and Other Crafts

The Spanish called the green beads they received from the Indians in strings as gifts **piedra de ijada** which translated literaly means "loin stone". They believed that the mineral of this stone possessed the power to cure back and kidney disorders. Our word "**jade**" in English comes from **ijada**.

"The stone which they call **piedra de ijada** and which would appear to belong to the better class of emerald, is usually green in color flecked with white. The better stones are those which are dark green. The Indians have used them since ancient times and wear them in many ways. In some instances, they have been cut into the shape of fish or birds,heads or even parrot bills. Others are simply round. The natives bored holes in them so that they could wear them to cure backache or stomach pains as they believed that the stone was endowed with the special powers to do so."

In Campeche, Juan de Grijalva's men received gifts of (items) of gold and likewise, Hernán Cortés received gifts from Moctezuma when he was about to launch his attack on Tenochtitlán from Veracruz.

Fray Juan de Torquemada spoke of the skill of the Indian gold and silversmiths and of the richness and originality of their work. "They were very adept in the arts of melting and casting gold and silver and produce fine pieces of jewelry in these metals. Our Spanish jewelers benefited greatly from watching them make a bird, the head, wings and tail of which moved. They also made a monkey and another animal which they attached to it so that they appeared to be dancing together. As well as these marvelous pieces, they produced another which was made half of gold and half of silver and this was much admired by our silversmiths from Spain."

Copper, which was scarce, was worked in the same way as gold and silver. To remove copper oxide from the surface of gold pieces, it was dissolved in a solution of vegetable acids.

Gold was chiefly used to make religious artifacts rather than in the production of personal accessories. The processes used by the Mayans involved the application of gold plate to a copper base, lamination and embossing. Oxides were used to color the metals. Platinum has only been discovered in the southern Andes, in Colombia and in northern Ecuador. Gold and silver were not used by the Mayans as currency.

The Mayans did not show much interest in gold and silver but they did, however, recognize, their maleable, ductile qualities and their resistance to oxidization as well as of course, as we have said, their natural beauty. It is very unusual to find metal pieces under the steles, in tombs and on altars. The pieces which have been found tend to be smaller items such as bracelets, rings, rattles, liprings and beads made from low grade gold. They are, nevertheless, valuable for their fine designs and filigree work. Alloys used include almost pure gold, and copper mixed with tin and arsenic. Some outstanding pieces are the discs of gold showing the heads of a Mexican god and a bird of prey which are inlaid with copper. These were found at the ruins at Zaculeu (Huehuetenango, Guatemala) and they belong to the **Mam** or **Mame** culture.

Also worthy of note are the nine golden rattles discovered during the restoration of the ruins of Mixco Viejo in 1959 (Chimaltenango, Pokomam culture).

Clay beads covered with gold have been uncovered in various parts of the ancient Mayan empire. The techniques employed in making them remains a mistery as the layer of gold is very thin and there are no signs of any joins. The scarcity of metal objects found in the southern and western Mayan areas (Guatemala and Honduras) leads us to the conclusion that despite the qualities of metal, it did not surplant stone as the most important medium. In addition, most of the pieces which have been found are of foreign origins.

The substitution of European ways for the ways of the indigenous culture meant that the mines were abandoned and the natives soon forgot about jade which in earlier days had been considered beautiful enough to be offered as a gift to gods and kings.

Apart from jade, actinolite, onyx, albite, beryl, chlorite, jasper, malachite, serpentine, etc., were known and used by the Mayans. These semi-translucent minerals were used in larger pieces such as the steatite vase from Kaminal-

A jade breastplate from Nebaj. Museum of Archaeology and Ethnology, Guatemala.

Juyú and the sculpture in muscovite from Uaxactún which belongs to the Tzacol age.

Xolotlán, Maxtlán and Tehuantepec which are the neighboring territories of the Mayans, paid tribute to the Aztecs with jade. The invaders of these areas judged this to be fine plunder as they spread from the Aztec empire to Honduras and Nicaragua.

Jade is one of the hardest nephrites known (6.5 to 6.8 on the scale used by geologists to classify rocks) and so is difficult to work with. The Mayans, however, used ingenious methods which are very worthy of praise.

Using obsidian chisels and a length of twine to guide the cuts of the chisel and jade or quartz dust mixed with water, they were able to engrave and cut the mineral to produce pieces, the perfection of which is admirable. An outstanding example of work in jade is the piece from Nebaj which is the most valuable item in the collection housed in the Museum of Archaeology and Ethnology in Guatemala. Likewise, the Leyden Plaque from an estele in Tikal (320 AD) is a beautiful slab of green which is engraved with glyphs on one side and on the other with the profile of a god holding a ceremonial staff in his arms. The plaque of carved jade which is in the British Museum, depicts a **Ha-**

lach Uinic on a raised platform with his body facing forwards and his head in profile.

The Mayans followed the general lines created by their sense of the esthetic in architecture, sculpture and painting, using graceful curves and frets which came to form their trademark.

"In the presence of reality, their creations were governed by an ideological symbolism in which the supernatural, the fantastic, the tremendous and the monstruous almost always figure. Therefore, most of the items produced by the gold and silversmiths and the craftsmen working in stone, were not inspired by the subject itself but by a mythical feeling searching for expression in a magical world which we find difficult to understand and evaluate even though at times the figures of gods and animals capture an astounding air of reality, highlighting the skill of the artist.

"Indigenous art is not generally something within the immediate understanding of those used to European expressions of art. When looking at examples of these exotic gold and silver pieces, the observer is most generally astounded by the feeling of love embodied in the creation. This is particularly evident if one takes into consideration the fact that they are the product of a race which, despite its efforts, was unable to develop a level of technology comparable to that of their contemporaries in Asia and Europe." (Samayoa Chinchilla.)

Other Arts and Crafts

Most of the baskets and hampers made in Central America, Chiapas and the Yucatán today derive from the old indigenous traditions of handcrafts.

Baskets, **toles**, bags, boxes, bread-baskets decorated and plain, and **chiquihuites** are all every day items which, as well as being functional, are also a form of artistic expression.

Our only guide to the artifacts which were hand-held or carried on the heads of Mayan women is provided by the reliefs and figures of the First Empire. The baskets woven nowadays like those made by the Landondan Indians for example, are crude and unremarkable, having degenerated like other many art forms after the collapse of the great Mayan civilization.

Impressions left by baskets have been found in the clay or cement floors of tombs and under the foundations of buildings. The design of the weave of the basket base is

Baskets sculpted on lintels at Yaxchilán, Chiapas, Mexico.

still distinguishable but their shapes and motifs can only be admired in the bas-reliefs and sculptures.

In Yaxchilán, Mexico, there is a carving of a very elaborately worked basket, with fret-work round the middle, spaced by little squares. Another basket is visible on the Nebaj vase and its edge is worked in an arrow-like design. Both of these date from the Classic Mayan Period.

Men, women and children used baskets, hampers and **chiquihuites** to carry the earth and mortar used to build channels and other defences against man and the elements, dykes, Mayan highways and even the huge pyramids. This was the basic function of those humble utensils which played a very effective part in the construction of larger works of art.

The glyph used to represent a woven mat or bedroll when placed next to the symbol for the sun refers to **pop**, the first month of the Mayan calendar. Those who were in positions of authority, of a civil, military or religious nature, are shown seated on a mat during meetings or assemblies and because of this, the word for "mat" became synonomous with the concept of authority.

There are only vague traces of drawings and outlines of mats left. Like the fans used to blow fires and fans made from palm leaves decorated with feathers used by the **Halach Uinic**, these mats have long since returned to the earth whence they came.

It is supposed that since the mats were symbols of the hierarchy, they must have been elaborately decorated. In the Books of **Chilam Balam**, "mat" and "throne" are synonyms.

Mosaics

Mosaics are an especially fine expression of Mayan art and date from before the Classic Period. These early mosaics were made from chips of jadeite. Later, turquoise was used in Chiapas, and jade, jadeite and shell were used in Guatemala.

At the bottom of the **cenotes** in the Yucatán, pieces and fragments of these stones have been found, as well as in Kaminal Juyú Uaxactún, Tikal and in other areas of El Petén. Pieces of mosaic have also been discovered.

In the records of Fray Bernardino de Sahagún, we read of how "the masons worked with crystal, amethyst, rough emeralds or jade and turquoise using tempered copper tools and emery to shape them".

Later Sahagún tells us how semi-precious stones were worked with chisels made of obsidian and polished with emery before being mounted and stuck in place with a gum called **tzauhtli:** "They scraped them with flint and made them hollow. Then they bored them with a small copper tube. Next they cut the stones with great care, polished them and made them shine brilliantly and radiantly. After this, they were mounted on wood and were polished again with a very fine sand. One final polish finished the process." In Mayan mosaics, turquoise provided the blue tones; jade and malachite, green; coral, red; shells, white and pink; black from obsidian and pyrite; and gold was used for yellows.

There are examples of this noble art in museums in America and Europe. Despite the fact that the Mayans often used mosaic work to decorate vases, teeth, pitchers, shields, skulls, sceptres, masks, musical instruments and, of course, their idols, there are relatively few examples left.

Of course there may exist a lot more mosaics which have yet to be uncovered. Despite their lack of abundance, marvelous examples exist at Kaminal Juyú, Piedras Negras and Tikal. There are four discs from Chichén Itzá and three more from the substructure of the "Castle," Chichén Itzá; shells with jade mosaic work from Kaminal-Juyú; a human figure made of slivers of jade and turquoise, shell and jade earrings from Tikal. A mask inlaid with jade, obsidian and shell recovered from the tomb in the Temple of Inscriptions, Palenque, can be seen in the National Anthropology Museum in Mexico City.

Examples of mosaics on sculptures include the multicolored jaguar from the Pyramid of the Castle, Chichén Itzá and the jaguars guarding the steps to the temple at Copán.

Funeral mask of jade, mother of pearl and obsidian found in the tomb of the Temple of Inscriptions, Palenque, Chiapas. National Museum of Anthropology, Mexico City.

Most of the known mosaics are to be found on shields, helmets and breastplates — all battle dress. A wood and turquoise panel was found at Chichén Itzá, earrings with suns on them at Uaxactún, as well as vases, masks, helmets, sacrificial knives, and other ceremonial items.

Mosaics have also been found belonging to the Mayan, Zapotec, Olmec, Toltec and Aztec cultures.

Feathers

Given the perishable nature of feathers, there is very little left of the magnificent feather work of the Mayans. Of the surviving examples, however, the exceptionally fine headdress of plumes belonging to Moctezuma and sent as a gift to Charles V has been discovered — it can be viewed at the Imperial Museum in Vienna.

The plume of Moctezuma II restored in 1596 in Vienna is like a large fan, the feathers of which are about 87 cm. long. Round its base are fringes woven from lilac hummingbird down, cinnamon and pink heron down and it is decorated with half-moons and little half-moons of goldplate. The rest of it is made from purple macaw and humming bird feathers. This exotic piece is housed in the collection at the Quinquagenany Museum in Brussels. Other examples include the Mexican feather mosaics in the Escorial, the Pitti collection in Florence, the ceremonial shields in Stuttgart and the helmets at the Museum of Natural History in Vienna.

The Toltecs were great practioners of this art and they passed their sacred secrets down from father to son. They wove and sewed the feathers onto cotton to create plumes and diadems.

Colored designs appear on others with the figures outlined in black down and filled in with multi-colored feathers. Hemp was often used instead of cotton as a backing.

The patterns include geometric and animal (both totemic and heraldic) designs which belonged to the religious and military hierarchy. There are examples of marvelous birds from Guatemala, Chiapas, Honduras and the Yucatán — humming birds, herons, tucans, macaws, parrots, paraqueets, orioles, woodcocks, cardinals, eagles and **gipaetos**, as well as that most beautiful of birds which flies between the mountains and heaven — the sacred quetzal, messenger of the gods. Backgrounds and white tones were created from the down of ducks living in the lakes, lagoons, marshes and pools of the Mayan world.

Feathers were used for decorational purposes and also as emblems during great ceremonies by the military and religious leaders of the Mayans. They also adorned pieces of cane and wicker work, weapons and were worn as necklaces, tassles, bracelets, belts, crests and ceremonial objects. Feathers were also worn in pierced noses, figured in

Small figure carved from the bone of a stag. This piece is believed to have come from Palenque, Chiapas, Mexico.

skin paintings and were sewn on cloths, **chalchihuites**, rattles and natural flowers.

According to S.G. Morley, "one of the most impressive pieces of feather work is the plume worn by the **Halach Uinic** in panel number three at the ceremonial site of Piedras Negras.

"A crest of stiff feathers rises above the headdress out of which sticks the plume itself. The underside of the feathers can be seen where the plumes rise out of the crest, turned over in gracious curves. These feathers could only have come from the tail of the quetzal and were worn exclusively by the great leaders of the Mayan people.

"A similar headdress is worn by the **Halach Uinic** on stele 12 (Piedras Negras). In this case, the plume rises out

Richly colored plumes were often used in headdresses and for personal ornamentation by the Mayans. Design from a relief in the Temple of the Cross, Palenque, Chiapas, Mexico.

of the same type of rigid crest of feathers as in the previous example and once again the feathers used are quetzal feathers to which tufts of other feathers have been fixed, floating gracefully in the light breeze. This **Halach Uinic** is also wearing a very elegant short cape of feathers which falls lightly from his shoulders. The light floating treatment of the representation of the feathers lending the relief a sumptuous air of great distinction, is worthy of note.

"Another headdress of plumes which is probably more elaborate, but less elegant, is the one worn by the **Halach Uinic** standing up on stele 10 at Ceibal (south Petén). The feathers on this headdress fall more formally than those of the previous examples, although they do convey a sense of movement and airiness between the individual feathers."

"The techniques of this art appear to have been cruder during the New Empire and it is probable that during the final days of the Empire, this form of Mayan art fell into a state of permanent decadence like other forms of art with the notable exception of architecture. Rather mediocre examples of plumes of the New Empire appear on the wooden lintels of the Temple of the Jaguars at Chichén Itzá. Here the feathers appear heavy and as if carved by novices although it is difficult to determine whether this is due entirely to inferior techniques or to a decline in the levels of craftsmanship in carving."

The throne of the Lord of Gumarkah (of the Quiché Mayan culture) is said to have been very beautiful given the splendid canopy of plumes which shaded it and lent it an air of majestic sumptuousness.

At the beginning of the sixteenth century, the Quichés, Cakchiqueles, Pokomames and Pokomichies were accustomed to sending great quantities of colored feathers to the major centers on the Mexican plains.

Flint and obsidian

Mayans used flint and obsidian as they lacked hard metals. These minerals and rocks were used from the Classic Period onwards to make knives, axeheads, chisels, spatulas and even needles which were all commonly used in daily life. Lance heads, arrows and darts used in war were also fashioned from flint and obsidian.

There are many of the blocks of stone which were shaped by chiseling or abrasion. Those craftsmen who worked with stone were able to shape a piece of flint with four or five well-placed blows which they then refined further by rubbing it down and polishing it until the desired form was finally produced.

In the foundations of high walls and under steles and altars, it is quite common to find small flint shapes which are beautifully crafted and pieces of engraved obsidian.

The fragments that have been recovered from Kaminal Juyú (late Pre-classic) are plain without any engraving and were only worked on four or five faces.

It is thought that the Mayans possibly adopted the same technique used by the Assyrians and the Egyptians to work large blocks of stone. This was done by making a series of holes in the stone and then placing pegs of hard wood in them. These were then soaked causing them to expand and split the stone in the desired place.

Obsidian was used to make knives, chisels, scalpels, offerings and ornaments. Obsidian is a type of volcanic glass found in abundance in areas of high land and is relatively uncommon at sea level. Thus, the buying and selling of obsidian was quite an active business between the communities on the plains and in the coastal areas.

By exerting great pressure on the lumps of obsidian and breaking it into splinters, the Mayans obtained oval shaped slivers called **chayes** which were shaped like laurel or iris leaves. The edges of these splinters were very sharp and suitable for use as razor blades, arrow heads, knives and for decorational purpose.

Along with aventurines, jadeite and iron pyrites, obsidian was also used in making masks, mirrors and for decorative ends.

The system of putting convergent or conical perforations in objects comes from the Mayan and Mexican cultures. A piece with three men's heads in profile was found in Quiriguá and beautiful offerings in flint and engraved obsidian were found at Tikal.

Stamps, markers and ink rollers were generally made from baked clay and were used to print designs and signs on human skin, material, paper and ceramic pieces.

There are a great many of these objects to be found all over the Mayan region as they were mass produced using molds. Flat and cylindrically shaped stamps were for printing on flat surfaces and concave or convex stamps for curved areas.

The Mayans used stamps right from the very earliest times and markers were popular during the Classic Period. Of the pieces found, measurements vary from 2 or 3 inches wide to 9 or 10 inches long. The patterns on them are delicate and pretty, chiefly figuring ears of corn, eagles, skulls, scrolls, frets and arabesques.

Grooming and Apparel

The following is a description of the land Christopher Columbus called Catay (the northern coast of Honduras) which the High Admiral wrote in a letter to the rulers of Spain. This letter constitutes the first reference to the dress of the natives: "It is said that there are great copper mines there and the people make axes and other articles from this material as well as from silver. In that land, the people are clothed and their garments consist of large cotton sheets with fine embroidery worked on them — others are painted very subtly in many colors. It is reported that further inland towards Catay, they have materials woven with gold."

According to Bernal, Landa and Sahagún, "The clothes of the Indians (the men) consist of a strip of material which measures about a hand's breadth. This serves as knickers and breeches. They wind this strip around the waist a few times with the ends hanging at the back and the front. Usually, these ends are worked very meticulously with feather-work by the women. They also wear long square sheets fixed at the shoulders. On their feet, they wear hemp or deerskin sandals. Apart from what is described here, they use no other form of clothing.

"The women pierce their noses through the central cartilage in order to place adornments of amber in the hole which they wear on special occasions. Like their husbands, the women also pierce their ears and wear earrings. They cover their bodies from the waist up (not those who are breast feeding) with designs which are finer and more beautiful than those of the men. Both men and women are accoustomed to washing themselves regularly with cold water and the women are not generally modest about this as they are used to undressing when they go to the well for the water.

Tzontil Indian weaving a huipil.
San Andrés Larraizar, Chiapas, Mexico.

"Like their husbands, the women smear themselves with a colored ungent and put on a sticky, perfumed gum which I believe to be amber oil. They call it **iztah-té** and to apply it to their bodies, they pour it on a decorated stone with which they rub themselves all over.

"The women wear their hair long and in very elaborate styles with a center parting and two braids. When girls are about to get married, their mothers prepare them with so much care that I have seen as many Indian girls with peculiar hairstyles as Spanish girls. Until a girl is adult, she generally wears her hair in either two or four bunches and this style suits them very well."

(On the coast of Chiapas, they put oil of **napahuite** on their hair to make it shiny and soft — in particular, it is applied to the long braids of the girls.)

"The Indian girls from the costal regions of Bacalar and Campeche are very modest in their manner of dress — as well as covering themselves from the waist down, they also wear garments to cover their breasts. This garment consists of a piece of folded material fastened under the arms. Other women normally just wear a sack-like dress, open at the sides and fixed at hip level. This is the only clothing they possess apart from a sleeping sheet which they carry with them during the day, folded up."

Jade, clay, metal, bone, shells and feathers were very often used to adorn earrings, necklaces, chokers, bracelets, breastplates and belts. Plumes of quetzal and macaw feathers were also used for decorational purposes. Important figures in Mayan society hoarded teeth which they had decorated with small jade discs or iron pyrite. Leaders and witch doctors commonly tatooed their faces and chests.

We can see how the Mayans of the Classic Period adorned themselves in the paintings and sculptures from this period — generally the people dressed carefully and elegantly. Designs were geometric made up of astronomical symbols, plants, flowers and animals. Brocade and lace were known and textile arts probably reached great peaks despite the fact that we have little left of actual garments as time and the atmosphere have destroyed, for example, the cloths in which bodies were wrapped when they were laid to rest in the tombs. Pieces of cloth which were recovered from the **cenote** at Chichén-Itzá (they were preserved by the mud) confirm this hypothesis, however.

When the end dawned for the Mayans with the Conquest the Indians on the coast went about half-naked. In the uplands where it is a lot colder, they wore more clothes.

Defeated, the natives began to mix elements of their indigenous dress with those of the Spaniards. This can also be attributed to the missionaries who awakened feelings of modesty among the Indians as far as dress is concerned — a western trait.

In his book "The Greatness and Decadence of the Mayan Indians," Thompson says, "the designs we see today adorning the blouses or **huipiles** of the Mayan women from the uplands would appear to be embroidered. They are in fact, brocade — the designs are worked in the warp to measure when the length of material is woven. It is very probable that this is an old Indian technique.

"Another equally old technique which we are aware of involves tying parts of the finished material very firmly at intervals and then immersing it in dye. In this way, the pieces which re tied do not absorb any color.

"Tapestry was as common among the Mayans (in particular among the Gobelinos of Chichicastenango) as it was in old Peru. Quilting was also practised and continued throughout the early days of the Conquest in the uplands of Guatemala. Percale is still woven by the Kekchíes and the early Spanish writers describe clothes made of feathers which were worn by the nobility — this observation is substantiated by many of the Mayan sculptures.

"For the Mayan women, weaving was as sacred a task as cultivating the land which was the domain of their menfolk. To this day, the women of Guatemala continue to offer up prayers before beginning to weave. There is also a social aspect attached to weaving in that the women of the Yucatán gather together in a building specially built for this purpose.

"Twine, netting and bags for carrying things like clothing were commonly made of hemp and **ixtli**. It is probable that in the rural communities, the people did not normally wear many clothes and we have reason to believe that only members of the governing class wore garments made of cotton. Fabric made from tree bark painted with designs was sometimes used for making clothes as well as the fibers of certain plants — in particular, the wild fig. To soften the fibers, they used to soak them and then beat them until flexible. Any holes which appeared in the "cloth" were patched by hammering on other fibers while the fabric was still fresh and damp. Clothes made of vegetable fiber are still worn by the Lacandón Indians and it is common to find specially shaped stones which it is believed were used to pound the fibers."

Despite certain changes, the clothing worn by the Indians today, is very varied and colorful. In general, men's clothing is made from wool and cotton, and cotton and many hues of silks are used for the clothes of the women. The feathers, gold and silver have disappeared but the richness and good taste remain.

The colors favored today still reflect Mayan symbolism — black for mourning is also representative of violence and evokes images of obsidian and wood timbered by fire; yellow is the color of corn — the Mayan's daily bread, and blue is representative of the sacrifices made to encourage the benevolence of the gods. Red is blood and green is wealth conjuring up images of the lushness of jungle vege-

Festive dress. Tizimín, Yucatán Mexico.

tation and the green of the quetzal feathers, symbol of the nobility.

Without any doubt, the most attractive item of clothing worn by the women is the **huipil**. And there are variations to suit every occasion — for going to mass, to weddings and, of course, the sisterhoods all have their own. All are richly colored and decorated with totemic designs which also incorporate some elements of European influence.

Some of the designs on the **huipils** represent the sun, the moon, the rains, lightening, language and the mountains. There is a large variety of **huipils** to be found in Mexico and Guatemala.

A "marrimba". This instrument is played by the Quiché Indians from Guatemala.

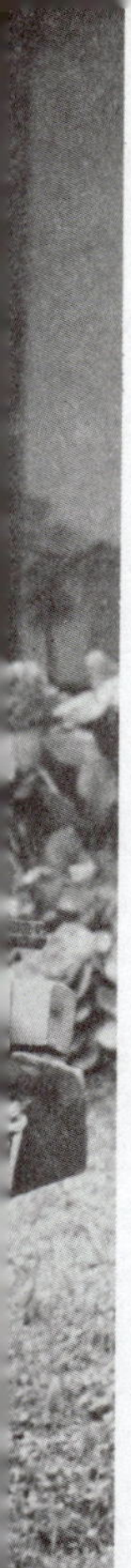

Music

There is very little Mayan music left in existence as unfortunately most of it suffered the same fate as the works of literature.

Nevertheless, a considerable variety of musical instruments have been found at the sites of the ruins. Along with these instruments, we can also get a good idea of what their music was like from paintings, sculptures and the writings of Landa, Lizana, Cogolludo and Sahagún.

Fray Diego de Landa had the following to say on the subject, "The Indians have very refined pastimes which in the main comprise farces which they perform with great poise. They are proficient enough for the Spaniards to hire them to act out scenes of them with their girlfriends or husbands or just them themselves, or on topics such as good and bad service. The Mayans perform these scenes with skill and much curiosity.

"They have small timbrels which they play with their hands. Others are made from hollow sticks which produce a melancholy, sad sound and are beaten with a long stick with (solidified) sap at one end." (This was a form of drumstick not unlike those used to play the marimba, the keys of which are made from the wood of the quira tree and comes from Guatemala. The sound of the marimba can be either sad or happy and can imitate the sounds of the jungle such as the roar of the jaguar or tropical storms, the warbling of birds, the singing of rivers or the lament of the Indian soul which sobs as it sings.)

"They have long, slim trumpets which are made out of hollow sticks. At the ends of these, they place long, twisted calabash. There are also some other instruments which are made out of whole tortoises, shell and all. What they do with these is scoop out the flesh of the animal and when they beat the hollow shell with the palm of the band, it produces a lugubrious, sad sound." (These small tortoise-shell drums are still played today during festivities in Guatemala. They are mainly seen at the **posadas** (Christmas parties) when the journey of the Holy Family is remembered along with the birth of Christ. They are simply called "tortoises" and are played alternately with the **posadas** or flageolet, the **tun** which is a little drum, timbrels or **chinchines** (made out of gourds and small hollow calabash) and other instruments.)

"Whistles and flutes made from sugar cane, deer bones and conch shells were also popular for making musical sounds.

"Two dances are especially impressive to see. One is called the "Cane Game" or **Colomché**, as the Mayans call it. To play, the dancers form a circle and then two of them go into the center. One holds a handful of darts and dances upright while the other dances, squatting down holding a stick to ward off the darts that the other aims at him.

"When the dancer has thrown all his darts, the two return to the circle and two others take their place in the center to repeat the game.

"Another dance needs eight hundred people or more to participate and they wave small flags in time to music recreating the atmosphere of war. During the dances nobody is permited to leave the circle. Mayan dances are generally long, tiring affairs lasting all day. Consequently, food and drink is provided. The men and women do not usually dance together."

Mayan percussion instruments, drums with one or two heads, whistles, timbrels, rattles, scrapers, flutes, ocarinas, trumpets etc, were made out of a wide variety of materials which included human bones. They used anything that would reproduce the sounds of nature.

The Mayans sang to their gods and danced for the divinities in order to "ensure their help in the divine tasks of giving life and birth to the world and to help invoke or avoid the dark forces of the unknown. Music was rarely made to express human love and death in these ancient displays of emotion."

Music was and continues to be the artistic expression of the soul and customs of the indigenous communities, integrating vast, marvelous musical geography of Guatemala and the area inhabited by the Mayans of the First Empire in the Yucatán. Their music is a steeped in sweetness and melancholy.

Remains of purely musical works can be found scattered in isolated parts of the Mayan world. Not so much is left in

A decorated clay Mayan whistle.

places where the Indians were in contact with the white man. Furthermore, it is very difficult to distinguish between the elements of Spanish influence and the purely Indian elements. Thus it would be true to say that cross-breeding also occured in the musical world.

Dancing and singing are mixed in with the indigenous music. During ceremonies where music was played, political leaders, priests, acolytes and the ordinary people all took part.

From the historians of the time, we learn that lead singers called **Hol-pop** existed in Mayan society and it was their duty to lead the chorus, teach music, sing and conduct. The flute, trumpet, tortoise drum players and the **teponahua** players were called the **ah-pax**. Others dedicated their time and efforts to composing songs and hymns of both a religious and warlike nature.

On a cup found at Chamá, dating from the Post-classic Period we see four men disguised as animals playing timbrels, a little drum and a tortoise shell drum which is being beaten with a piece of staghorn. The murals at Bonampak also provide information about Mayan music — in one of them, there are sixteen musicians playing the instruments already described as well as a form of long, wooden trumpet.

The drum **(tun-kul)** and the **teponaxtle** (its Mexican name) are among the most important ancient artifacts discovered. Percussion instruments played the principal part in the war marches and funeral ceremonies. The voices of the Mayans were rythmical and lusty although tinged with sadness and apathy. The **tun-kul** was made from wood which gave it a resonant sound and in some cases it was made out of clay. The warmth of wood, however, produced an instrument with richer tones.

Musicians playing rattles and a jaguar skin drum. Bonampak, Chiapas. Copy in the National Museum of Anthropology, Mexico City.

Deer, jaguar and wild boar hides were used in making drums **(parche)**. In ancient times there was also a drum made from clay which is still played today by the Lacandón Indians. Their name for this instrument is **kayún**. Illustrations of drummers appear in the Dresden codex and, in the hieroglyphics, we learn of water drums. These drums had a hole in them and different levels of water produced different sounds.

The **tum** of the Quiché Indians, or the **teponaxtle**, is a drum played horizontally and it is made of wood split at either end with a piece in an "H" shape inserted into these splits. This instrument was played with the fingers or with drumsticks and was used to transmit messages through the woods or during war celebrations and religious and magical rites.

Wooden or clay drums were played with the fingers or with drumsticks producing rich, musical sounds. Franz Blom says, "the drumhead is made of the hide of the **baatz** or the great howler monkey, the great ape of the jungle hunted by the Mayans for food. In the **Popol Vuh**, the **baatz** and the **chouén** predominate in scenes of dancing and singing." (Hunbatz and Hunchouén were the brothers of the heroes Hunahpú and Ixbalanqué who scorned them and changed them into grotesque, gesticulating, howling monkeys. Prior to this, they had been very fine artists.)

Trumpets were used by the Mayans and originated from the age-old conch horns — putting a hollow tube on to them increased the volume of sound. Generally they were very long instruments as can be seen from the murals at Bonampak. Some measured almost two meters long and were made of wood or sugar cane covered in plaster, clay and palm leaves. Since they were played by the hierarchy or priests, they were often decorated with ribbons, multicolored plumes and glyphs.

The Quiché Mayans blew them in combat as testified by the "Cakchiquele Anals" also known as "The Tecpán Atitlán Records".

"They descended at the first light of day (reference to the battle between the Indians of Tibacoy and Rayakán) from the hills with great shouts and war cries, their flags unfurled and playing drums, trumpets and conch horns.

"The descent of the Quiché people was truly terrible. They advanced rapidly and were visible stretching into the distance, one behind another, on and on, coming down the mountain where they quickly arrived at the banks of the river and the houses built there. Tepepul and Iztayul (their leaders) came behind with their god (a false god of fratricidal war). The battle was horrific, accompanied by great shouts and cries, the beating of drums, trumpets and horns ringing on the air and blending with the enchantment of the heroes. Finally, the invading Quichés were fended off leaving behind many dead. Most of them fled without fighting.

"Many were taken prisoner including the kings, Tepepul and Iztayul who fell along with their god. **Galel Achi**, the **Rajpop Achí**, the grand-son and son of **Galel Achí**, were also taken. They were all put to death and so great was the death toll that the people of El Quiché did not know how many had died at the hands of the Cakchiqueles." (The Cakchiqueles were a very belicose people and sworn enemies of the Quichés with whom they shared their origins. They had helped Alvarado in taking the great Quiché bastions by storm and destroying their settlements.

The trumpets of the Classical Period survived until the days of the colonization. The historian, Captain Francisco Antonio de Fuentes y Guzmán says that the natives constantly demanded that they be allowed to dance the **Oxtum** dance. This is accompanied by the sound of long ebony trumpets, **teponaxtles**, conch horns and flutes.

The Mayan flute (**xul**) had a large mouthpiece and produced a pleasant sound. Both straight and globular flutes were typical.

The flute known as the Lacandon oboe is really more like a flageolet—at one end, it had a piece of bird bone fixed in place with wax and this acted as the mouthpiece of the instrument.

Flutes were made from reeds, clay, jade and bones, including human bones. A four-holed instrument made from a child's femur was uncovered during the excavations at Guatemala. This was the site of Ixmiché during the late Post- classic Period.

Flutes were commonly played in combinations of two or more so that several notes could be produced at one time. On the island of Jaína in Campeche, a flute was found which reproduces the seven notes of the European diatonic scale. In pictures of groups of musicians in Guatemala, we can see that they are playing what look like piccolos or **tzicolaj**.

A Lacandón oboe was discovered by Franz Blom proving that even today we are still using traditional scales despite being aware of a greater range of notes. Blom's oboe has seven holes, unlike the Jaína flute which only has six, and it is capable or producing eight different notes. A series of seven tones were produced using the tube of the "oboe". Unable to make full use of this extensive range of tones, musicians used to plug the seventh hole with wax and just make use of the seven basic notes of a traditional scale.

The Mayans used maracas a lot in their music and these instruments were believed to be endowed with magical powers. Painters and sculptors depict them as being attributes of the divine along with pouches of copal resin and other voluntary offerings in the codices and sculptures.

Maracas which were worn as earrings have been found along with others in the form of ceremonial staffs or cylindrical objects which were significant in agricultural rites and for invoking the rains. Examples made of clay, wood, gold, silver and copper have been found as well as others made from small gourds. Generally the maracas are painted black and have a stick inserted into them to act as a grip. The noise was produced from the shaking of seeds, small stones or chippings inside. The maraca is still used extensively in the music of Mexico, the Antilles and Central America.

Whistles were a favorite instrument in the Mayan world and many have been discovered at the various archaeological sities. As well as being used to make music, the Mayans used them when hunting to attract small game, birds and animals. They come in various shapes and forms and produce a wide range of notes. Some were made in the form of simple antropomorphical and zoomorphical figures, in groups of two of three. The San Agustín Acasaguastlán piece found in Guatemala is very well-known. It dates back to the Classic-Period and is of a cro-

The Mayans used sea shells as musical instruments.

codile head with four holes. When the holes are covered either completely or just half-covered according to position of the fingers of the player, an octave ranging from F7 to F8 of the German acoustic scale can be produced.

Like the long flutes, the ocarina or round flute is distinguished from the whistles by the number of holes (used to augment or vary the pitch). Fewer examples of this instrument have been discovered. Another wind instrument was made of two connecting jars containing water. When the water was moved in one, long, unusual but nevertheless pleasant tones were emitted.

The scrapers which are grooved instruments perhaps originated in America first among the Olmecs. They were made from human and animal bones and were generally long in shape. The Indians played the scrapers during erotic festivals (not Mayan) or to pay homage to the dead. Examples appear in the Florentine and Viennese Codices as well as in the "Tribute Books" also known as the Mendoza Codex.

There are many references to the music and dances of the Quiché Mayans in the **Popol Vuh**. The musical instruments brought to the uplands of Guatemala by the people of Tula, Mexico are also mentioned.

Some researchers, working from Sahagún, hare noted that: "The importance of this form of art in the development of our people, their beliefs and religious practice and their views on life itself, has been vital.

"As Sahagún correctly observes, music is not confined to religion but formed an important element in erotic dances, ordinary dances and every day-life. All the historians of this culture have admired this unique skill of the Indians and their general artistic discipline.

"Their talents are further highlighted by the comparable ease with which they managed to adapt to Catholic hymns—this proves that their musical ability must have been inborn and hereditary. We have known about ritual objects, players, ceremonial flutes and compositions and dances for a long time now but, nonetheless, research is still very vague on the subject—very few thorough studies have been made. It is strange given the richness and attractiveness of this subject that so little serious research has been carried-out.

"The Indians do not dance and sing for their own diversion or adulation nor to show off their talents. For them, music is an expression of faith, hope and fear, a concept which compounds the difference with European music.

"Those who sing love ballads and songs of death (in other words, songs of a personal nature) are barely accorded any importance. On the other hand, the music of the ancient culture is so full of vitality that it is impossible to analyse the reasons for the assimilation of exotic rythms which lends them a certain degree of autochtonous interpretation.

"The musical instruments such as lutes, guitars and the violins of the Lacandónes, Chamulas, Otomíes and Tarahumaras are similar to the European concepts of these instruments during the sixteenth century. It is impossible, however, to play European music with them. Furthermore, it is not true that the Aztec scale consisted of five notes. We know this is not so given our knowledge of their compositions and other instruments which were very skillfully crafted such as the giant scraper from Oaxaca which incorporates trumpets, drums and four different types of grooves. The double and triple flutes are also very complex instruments.

"Pre-Conquest music can be described as magical, totemic or of a hunting nature. There is music for rituals, battles and even humorous ceremonial music which imitates the sounds of birds and animals. Profane music for entertainment also existed."

Mayan music also drew its inspiration from nature such as from the song of the birds like the **cenzontle** (flour hundred voices), the woodcock, and a host of others. The music of the ancient Mayans is characterized by the use of arpegios of sustained notes which alternate with rapid scales. Themes were regularly repeated and provoked sounds of undescribable nostalgia and melancholy. "These reflect the senstitive hearts of the people who gave life and splendor to the Mayan culture in primitive times."

Dance and Festivities

In a study of the dance called **Tum-Teleche** or **Loj-Tum** it was noted that the play **Rabinal-Achí** may be a variation of this dance known by the first of these names in other areas. In both the play and the dance, the main theme is that of a human sacrifice. To quote the words of the researcher, Among other interesting documents on the inquisition in Guatemala which are housed in the National General Archives in Mexico City, I had the opportunity to consult a report on the Indian dance called **Tum-Teleche** or **Loj-Tum**.

"This information was compiled in 1620 by the Commissary of the Holy Office in Mazatenango, Guatemala, R.P.D. Antonio Prieto de Villegas. In his report, it is very clear that the inquisition leaders attributed themselves certain jurisdiction over the Indian population and this jurisdiction was put into effect when they committed religious errors. Action was only taken, however, after a through investigation had been carried-out to determine the severity of the act of heresy.

"Let me warn Your Illustrious Lordship of two matters," wrote Prieto de Villegas in a letter sent to the Inquisition leaders in Mexico. "Firstly, it has been claimed by some that the Indians continue to practice their old superstitions which appear to contain some elements of idolotry.

"I consulted Dean don Felipe Ruiz del Corral, your Lordship's Commissary, on the matter and he replied that the Holy Office does not intend to take action against the Indians for the time being and will leave the punishment of such offences to the civil authorities. Bearing all this in mind, it occured to me that Your Lordship might be interested to know how these matters are being dealt with here if other cases against the Indians are brought forward which affect this Holy Tribunal.

A mask representing a Spanish Conquistador as used by the Indians from Todos los Santos Cuchumatanes, Guatemala, in their dance of the Conquest.

"...and so the dance continued to be performed until a short time later when the very same Prieto de Villegas was made Commissary of the Inquisition in Mazatenango. In 1624, he gave the orders for the carrying-out of a very severe **auto-de-fé** to erradicate the dance the Indians called **Tum-Teleche** in the communities under his control. His objection to the dance were that it enacted a sacrifice performed by the **Nahuales**."

This Mayan dance was mystical (as regards religion and **nahualism** or totemism) and warlike. There are only occasional vague references to it in paintings and carvings, in scraps of oral or written tales, and adulterated, damaged remains. It also survives in the ancient feelings like the Commandments of Christians. The sacrificial rites in honor of **Tohil** (the Moloch of the Mayan Pantheon) who was insatiably hungry for blood and human flesh, continued long after the Conquest.

Documents written by the Catholic clergy during the seventeenth century indicate that, "...it concerns an Indian who was sacrified as an offering to the devil after having been taken prisoner in battle. Whilst tied to a tethering post, he is attacked by the four **nahuales** who are going to take his life. These **nahuales** represent a jaguar, a puma, an eagle (**gipaeto**) and another type of unknown animal. Other movements and shrieks executed during this dance are accompanied by a blood-curdling, sad sound made by long, twisted trumpets which are similar to sackbuts. The sound of this instrument inspires terror among those who hear it. Furthermore, I have seen this dance performed in other towns and the people and even animals have been greatly upset by the sound of the trumpets. The agony of the sound affects them profoundly unlike in other **tum** dances which they must be used to."

During the Classic Mayan Period, human sacrifices were not carried out regularly. It was only after this period that such rites were incorporated into Mayan customs through the influence of invading tribes.

Bishop Landa, a chronicler of the Post-classic Period (after the Conquest) describes the form of a sacrificial ceremony: "...and when the day came, they gathered in the courtyard of the temple if there was a prisoner to be sacrificed and killed by arrow wounds. They would strip him naked, annoint his body with blue dye and place a crown upon his head. After the devil had danced a solemn dance with him for the people, all those who were armed with bows and arrows would dance round the pole to which he had been bound.

"Then a priest (warlock) in his ceremonial clothes would approach him and wound him in the stomach. From the

A human sacrifice which corresponds to the description made by Bishop Landa. From stele number 11 at Piedras Negras, Guatemala.

wound, he would draw blood with which he annointed the face of the devil."

Landa continues saying, "When a signal was given to the dancers, they quickly moved away and after the order had been given, they started to shoot arrows at the heart of the victim. Prior to this, the position of the heart had been marked with a white target. Thus, the victim was put to death, his chest like a hedgehog with spines of arrows."

The following is a description of a dance from the Yucatán region:

"...A missionary (at the beginning of the Viceroyalty) was welcomed with many dances... and during the course of one of them, the rejoicing Indians brought out a peculiar type of portable platform with a broad, round castle on top. This castle looked rather like a pulpit and was more than six feet high and was covered with lengths of painted cotton. Two flags flew from the top, one on each side.

"A well-dressed, elegant looking Indian was standing in the pulpit although only visible from the waist up. In one hand, he held a clay rattle and in the other, a feathered fly-swat. He was turned to face the Father Commissary and moved constantly whistling and accompanied by an Indian playing a **teponaxtle** at the base of the platform. Other Indians sang, made loud noises and whistled while this was going on.

"Six Indians bore the platform on their shoulders and they too danced and sang, shaking their feet and following the movements of the others to the sound of the **teponaxtle.** The castle was indeed a spectacular sight and was

Lacandon Indians from Najá; Chiapas, Mexico,during the Balché ceremonies. They are burning copal.

well-decorated with painted designs. Its height was also impressive. In the language of the Indians, they call the dance **zonó**. It dates from ancient times."

Landa claims to have been present at a dance in which 150 people took part, dressed in sumptuous attire. He says that the people flocked in their thousands to watch it.

During the first few days of the new year, a fire dance was performed on top of the smoking embers of a bonfire. "After raking the embers out evenly alongside those who had just danced, some Indians stepped forward and began to walk barefoot and naked over them. Some completed the task unharmed whilst others were scorched or half-burned. They believed that by doing this, their problems would be solved and the ill-omens they had witnessed would be abated. It was also thought to encourage the good-will of the gods."

Other examples of Mayan dances include the "Arrow Dance" **(cakbat-zulú)** which was basically a wardance. Another, called **naual** was very erotic. Both of these were suppressed along with others by the Catholic clergy given that they always culminated in an orgy.

Many animal dances are mentioned in the **Popol Vuh**: the **puhuy** (owl dance; also called **tucur**); **cux** (the weasel); the **iboy** (the armadillo); the **xtzul** (the centipede); the **chitic** (the wader bird); and the **hunahpú-coy** (the monkey).

Brasseur de Bourburg says that the **pachob** was the dance of lovers in the Yucatán and was danced until the latter part of the nineteenth century. The solemn dance of **zayí** (the tapir) was performed by old men holding flowering palms in their hands accompanied by very sedate music.

In the " Annals of the Cakchiqueles", mythical and war dances are described. One of these dances evokes the portent of Cabaguitz who contained an eruption of the Yaxcanul, great lord of the volcanoes.

The books of the **Chilam Balam** talk of a rite called **Kay-Nicté** (Song of the Flower). In it, the lover tries to attract an unfaithful woman whom he finds naked in the light of the moon. He wants her to dance with him as an act of homage to the gods and to implore them to give her back her indifferent partner.

Men and women had their own particular dances and very rarely did they dance together. ". . . Many dances needed the participation of over a thousand people and were performed on special occasions. These attracted large numbers of spectators—fifteen thousand Indians in some cases and included those who had travelled considerable distances to see these great spectacles."

The Mayans danced under the watchful eyes of the gods. For them, "ball games and dancing were merely two ways in which to express a joyful impulse in adoration and movement in honor of the mysteries and natural forces of Creation.

"Unlike modern man, the Mayans were not reasoned thinkers. Intellect did not intervene between their emotions and the expression of their emotions which was generally innocent and fatalistic. Thus, the Mayans threw themselves wholeheartedly into their dancing, singing and drinking (the weak point of these people) during religious celebrations. It was not their intention to seek artificial pleasure from these pursuits as man of today does — the Mayans acted spontaneously in the declaration of their feelings, the main objective of which was to honor their gods and interpret the universe."

Wrapped in splendid hues of green, in a state of trance, seeing mystical visions, naked and adorned with plumes or covered by monkey, jaguar or deer skins the priests, warriors and **chilanes** would dance from dawn to dusk, taking small, measured steps, their heads proud or bowed, brandishing bows, lances or clubs. They danced without even stopping to drink gourds of **balché** (a strong alcoholic beverage made from the bark of the hominy tree which was fermented with corn and wild honey) or to piously say their millenaires or prayers.

The dancers often wore masks to represent the gods and to beg for their protection during battles, fishing, hunting and other agricultural persuits. Masks were also worn to symbolise a passion or to identify with the totem, "in the spirit of dark eagerness to make the subconcious flourish."

Festivities were generally proceeded by periods of fasting and sexual abstinence which lasted for anything up to two weeks. Precision was of fanatic importance in their dances and for missing the beat, it is recorded that punishment in some cases was as severe as the death of the offender. It was also punishable not to interpret the words and spirit of the songs with the reverence demanded.

Almost all war celebrations and religious festivities ended with singing and dancing. Every month of the Mayan year had its own special celebrations. These celebrations have survived throughtout the ages and are re-enacted by societies involved in keeping alive the old traditions.

A **katun** was a twenty year period on the last thirteen days of which there would be celebrations. These festivities started in Uaxactún in 357 AD and were carried-out during twelve centuries. Each of the **katunes** had its own god and after a monument was erected in homage of the god marking a milestone in the history of the Mayans, there would be celebrations and festivities. The years **kan**, **muluc**, **ix** and **cauac** all had their own gods and forms of celebration. In general, Mayan months were shorter than ours today and consequently they had more than we do.

In accordance with the calculation of time, which was rather complicated, each month had its own particular ceremonies. For the new year (summer solstice) which fell on the sixteenth of July of our calendar, the gods **Bolón Tzacab** and **Kan U Uayeb** were praised. Incense was burned before their images and this was made of a mixture of cornstarch and **pom**. Before the dancing was concluded, a deer or a turkey would be offered as a sacrifice along with food and drink. The Mayans fasted for thirteen days during this month, relit the fires in their homes and replaced their house-hold utensils with new ones. Homes were given a thorough spring-clean and the four **chaces** or acolytes who aided the priests, would be solomnly chosen to serve during the following year.

The second month, **uo**, was dedicated to the worship of the protective gods of the **chamanes** or witch doctors. The gods who protected fishing and hunting were also remembered.

During **zip**, the third month, the luxuriously clothed priests would show and explain the sacred books to the people. They also made their prophecies in this month and the people danced before the image of the goddess **Ixchel** with their arms painted blue. They offered up the fruits of their hunting and fishing to this god.

In the fourth month, **zotz**, the guardians of the beehives started their preparations for the celebrations of the following month, **tzec**. They invoked the four **Bacabes** who were the celestial bee-keepers and were associated symbolically with the sacred colors and the points of the compass: red in the east; white in the north; black in the west; and yellow in the south. They burned incense and copal, drank agave juice and decorated plates and vessels with all sorts of bees.

The great festival for **Gucumatz (Kukulcán** in Mayan from Yucatán and **Quetzalcóatl** in the Mexican language) was celebrated in the month of **xul**. Long, lively processions wound their way to the temples and paraded the streets of the settlements. They offered up gifts of shells, jade and feathers and danced without stopping. The festival was called **Chic Kabán** and it was believed that on the last day, **Gucumatz** would descend from the skies to receive homage and offer protection to the people.

The general celebrations for all the gods started in the month called **yaxkín** — idols, spindles, emblems, weapons and household utensils were painted turquoise as were the hands of the young.

Mol was the month dedicated to making idols from **kuché** (cedar wood). The craftsmen worked in silence, keeping themselves shut away from the noises of day to day life. Incense was burned for the **Acantunes** who guarded the four points of the compass.

During the month of **chen**, these new idols were taken to the temples to be blessed. The priest sanctified the figures which were then handed out to the faithful who took them home and to the fields where they had planted their crops. They also danced, often for days at a time.

The favor of **Chac**, the rain god, was solicited during **yax**.

There was no dancing or any important celebrations during **ceh**.

The following month was called **mac** and, in this one, the elderly worshiped the four **chaces** by building pyres in the squares and temple porticoes. The priests tore the hearts out of jaguars and pumas and spilled their blood on the fires. The god **Tupp Kac** was praised and the entreaties of the people were to request water from the heavens. **Mac** coincided with the end of April and start of May — the time of year the farming cycle begins.

Kankín was a silent, celebration-free month.

Glyphs representing the "months" of the Mayan calendar which had 365 days. They had eighteen months of twenty days each except for one month which only had five days.

During **muan**, the festivities for the cocoa workers were held and **Chac** (god of rain), **Ek Chuah** (god of cocoa), and **Hobnil** (the **Bacab** of the **kan** years) were paid homage to.

A dog dyed the color of the husk of the cocoa bean was offered as a sacrifice along with gifts of jade, shells, feathers and blankets. Those participating in the celebrations drank chocolate and abstained from drinking alcohol.

The god, **Cit Chac Coh**, (Father of the Red Puma) was worshiped during **pax** and, the chiefs gathered before **Nacom** (Captain of War) to take him to the temple on a beautifully decorated platform covered in jewels and **chalchihuites**. They sacrificed a dog and offered its heart on two trays to **Cit Chac Coh**. This ceremony concluded when the **chaces** were each given a pitcher of wine and the dancing had stopped.

Chamula indians walking over hot coals during the purification rites of the Carnaval ceremonies. San Juan Chamula, Chiapas, Mexico.

Among the dances still performed by the Quiché Mayans are the dances of the deer, the joker and the snake. The Dance of the Deer represents the struggle between Man and beast and, given the ceremonial complexities of the dance, it is very spectacular to watch. The second one concerns mythology, time and fertility. The last one is about the eternal struggle existing between good and evil.

A great acrobatic dance appropriately named as the Dance of the Flying Pole, reenacts the conflict between Zipacná (he who raises the mountains) and the "four hundred boys" who were finally changed into a constellation of stars (the Pleiades) which is mentioned in the **Popol Vuh**. Some also believe this dance to be about the growing of corn.

The magnificent performers in this dance who put their lives at considerable risk by "flying" at great heights above

the ground, have to abstain from having sexual intercourse for two weeks before this wonderful spectacle.

"In some places in the Gulf area such as Papantla México and the Quiché region of Guatemala, they perform daring feats on the ends of swinging ropes attached to what is called the "Flying Pole." This is a marvelous sight and in ancient times was full of religious significance. In this context, hens, alcoholic beverages and other offerings were placed in the hole that the pole was stood in as it was felt that by making offerings, the gods would protect the performers from danger while "in flight." Before beginning their ascent of the pole, the ten men dance around the base of the pole wearing crowns (copilli) and blue and red kerchiefs on their heads. They also carry rattles, flutes and small drums.

"Near the top of the pole which is a robust mast, measuring approximately twenty meters in height, a rotating box with a narrow platform round it is situated. The coiled-up ropes (2 or 4) are attached to this platform.

"The first to climb up is the "monkey" wearing a wooden mask and a tail. This performer is a clown and it appears that his mission is to keep an eye on the uncoiling of the ropes. He sits on the platform and performs some acrobatics which demonstrate his expertise. He entertains the spectators thus until his companions have all followed him up the pole and attached themselves to the ropes. They then launch themselves into the air."

This dance is forbidden in some places in view of the unfortunate accidents that have ensued.

Leonar Schultze-Jena speaks of the prayer procession on the Mount of the Dead Souls (in Chichicastenango). He describes how four dancers fell asleep in the branches of a pine tree which is to be felled and of the banquet of the wood-cutters and their helpers. They set light to the tree which falls. Then the tree is blessed and two dancers are positioned at either end of it. The fate of the sleepers is at the hands of the woodcutters who were attracted to this particular tree as a propitiatory rite.

Curses are cast on evil spirits. It was belived that dwarves and hunchbacks were the sons of the sun and thus, were able to amuse the gods in some dances performed at times of eclipses. This explains their presence in murals and paintings in which they are seen dancing or lying before members of the hierarchy and figures of gods.

Theater

Knowing how fond the people of Mesoamerica were of theatrical productions, the missionaries who came to spread the word of Christ, made use of this fact.

In the dramatic arts and dances of the Mayans, the whole community had a part to play. These festivities were generally held in the open air in squares and temple porticoes and enlivened the celebrations for the **Katún** (a twenty year period), the beginning of a new cycle, highlights of the Mayan calendar, the close of a cycle during the months of **kayab**, **cumbú** and **uayeb**, for the consecration of new idols during the month of **mol**, and at the start and finish of the ball games.

There are numerous references to the theatrical arts in the chronicles but unfortunately, there are no original pieces left—almost all the works written were lost at the downfall of the Mayan world, either destroyed by the Conquistadores or swallowed up by the jungle. Only scanty remains of plays are left to us and these are mainly incomplete religious, historical and social works.

In Guatemala, however, a unique ballet-drama was miraculously saved from destruction. The play is about the Quiché Mayan, **Xapoj-Tun** otherwise known as **Rabinal-Achi** (the Man From Rabinal — a town which still exists in the Verapaz lowlands today).

The tales evolves around the battles which took place between the people of El Quiché and Rabinal.

Personal ornamentation contributed greatly to the staging of plays as we can see from the costume worn by this actor and dancer from the Yucatán.

Rabinal-Achí was discovered by Father Charles Etienne Brasseur de Bourburg to whom it was delivered orally. Father Charles wrote it down in 1856 after having it enacted by the Indians.

In this chapter, I shall endeavour to describe a part of this play, concentrating on its central stages.

Quiché-Achí (Quiché man) the captive warrior of the Rabinal people, has to appear before **Job-Toj**, the lord of Rabinal. He is accompanied by his son, **Rabinal-Achí** and the court. The scene takes place outside the city.

Quiché-Achí is judged and sentenced to be sacrificed, but before being put to death, he is allowed to return to his homelands in Gumarkah (called Santa Cruz de El Quiché by Bishop Francisco Marroquín which is the name by which it is known today). This is granted to him in deference to his social status. He is to say farewell to his people, mountains and valleys and after twenty days have passed thirteen times and twenty nights have passed thirteen times, **Quiché-Achí** returns to Rabinal to offer up his life as a sacrifice. He has given his word as a nobleman and leader to do this.

(Georges Reynaud says that apart from the unique personality of **Rabinal-Achí** which is probably his most remarkable quality, he has the peculiarity of constantly confirming and reinforcing the idea of balance or parallelism held by the Indians of Mesoamerica as regards their creation:

"Their buildings are geometrically balanced and balance is displayed in the codices in the way that columns of glyphs are placed next to drawings. This is also true of the inscriptions on the steles. They were balanced, logical thinkers as we can see from what remains of their writings in their tendency to repeat names, adjectives and even verbs. A system such as this makes it inevitable that their sentences revert to the roots of their ideas: for example actors repeat word for word what the previous speaker has just said before answering. In some instances, they even finish a sentence said by the speaker moments before. This is a feature readily found in primative literature — other examples can be found in the Bible, some old Arab texts, and in old Spanish texts dating from the sixteenth century. The technical term for this style is "antiphony".

Examples: The fan will descend from the sky; the garland of the sky will descend, the bouquet of the sky. They will find their harvest in the trees; they will find their harvest among the rocks, those people who lost their harvest during the **katún** of Noble II **Ahau**. The hills will burn; the valleys between them will burn. Fire will blaze in the great **sucté** tree. It will burn on the sea; on the sands. The seeds of the calabash will burn; the calabash will burn; the **macal** will burn.)

Beginning of the first act of Rabinal-Achí:

Characters: **Job-Toj**, Lord of Rabinal. **Rabinal-Achí**, his son. **Xocajau**, wife of Job-Toj. **Quiché-Achí**, prince of Cunén and Chajul. **Tzam-Kam-Carchah**, princess of Rabinal. Slaves, both male and female. Tiger nobles. Eagle nobles. The people of Rabinal.

The Palace of **Cakyug**. Twelfth century A.D. Internal war is being waged between the Quiché people of Gumarkah and Rabinal over the ownership of the district of Zamaneb. There is a wood in front of the palace. **Rabinal-Achí** and warriors are dancing to the tune of the **tunes. Quiché-Achí** appears, his lance at the ready.

Quiché-Achí (to **Rabinal-Achí**): Come here, perverse and haughty man! You are the first person I have been unable to defeat. You are the leader of the people of Chacachip, the people of Zamanip and Prince of Rabinal! Come here, I say! Stand before the sky and before the earth!

Rabinal-Achí takes up his rope of slip knots and flails it. He dances.

Rabinal-Achí: Oh, brave warrior, leader of El Quiché! You beg me to come forward and yet you call me perverse and haughty because you were unable to defeat me, the leader of the Chacachip, the Zamanip and Prince of Rabinal. Were not these your words? By the sky and the earth, you have certainly come to deliver yourself up to the point of my lance, to the power of my shield, or the blows of my mace, my axe, and my armbands of leather and metal; my magical herbs, my cotton tunic, my strength and my valor. If this be not so, I shall tie you up with my rope of white hemp. This I say to you before the sky and before the earth—may they look kindly upon you, brave man who is now my prisoner!

The music stops as does the dancing when **Quiche-Achí** is taken and bound.

Rabinal-Achí: Oh brave man, you are now my prisoner, before the sky and before the earth! Tell me, where are your mountains: where are your valleys? Were you born on the side of a mountain or on the slope of a valley? Are you a son of the clouds or a son of the mist? Did you flee from the point of my lance during the battle?

Quiché-Achí: By the sky and by the earth! Is this how you speak, uttering false words from your mouth before me? You call me brave and yet insinuate that I fled from the point of your lance in battle. come now! I am a truly brave man, would I really have fled from you? You ask about my mountains and my valleys, and I tell you that I am a brave warrior. I am son of the clouds and the mist, born in my mountains which rise higher than the sky and in my clouds which rise above the earth. This is all I will say. May the sky and the earth look kindly upon you, **Kalel-Achí, Rabinal-Achí**!

Rabinal-Achí: Ah, ha! Brave prisoner, you have not answered my questions; you have not told me the name of your mountains or the name of your valleys. You suppose that we know you were born on a mountain side, on the slope of a valley, and that you are the son of the clouds and of the mist. Is this not what you told us? These are vague answers. If you do not reveal the name of your mountains and the name of your valleys, I will drive you, bound with ropes to my Lord who sits within the walls of the great fortress, by the sky and by the earth! This, I can assure you, by the sky and the earth and may they look kindly upon you, prisoner! My captive!

Quiché-Achí: Damn the sky and damn the earth! You have said that you will find a way to make me reveal what you want to know and that if I do not tell you, you make threats saying that you will drive me bound with ropes before your Lord. These were your words as witnessed by the sky and by the earth. Oh, help me sky! Oh, help me, earth! To whom shall I tell the name of my mountains and the name of my valleys? To you, the birds of prey; to you, birds of brilliant plumage! I, a brave man; I, leader of the men of Cunén and the men Chajul. My great lord **Balam-Achí**, **Balam-Quiché** will certainly descend ten times from the depths of the clouds and the mist to my mountains and my valleys. This is all that I can tell you. From where will he descend; from where will his words be uttered, on the face of the skies and the earth? May they go with you, **Kalel-Achí**, **Rabinal-Achí**!

Rabinal-Achí: Oh, leader of the people of El Quiché! Oh, brave man! You claim by your origins to be my older brother, my younger brother. This is admirable. No doubt, my soul forgot seeing you or having watched you within the great walls of the fortress. It was you, of course, who imitated the howl of the wolf, the noises of the weasels, the roar of the jaguar on the walls of the fortress to frighten our young and to attract us to places where there is new golden honey, the food of our lord and leader, the old **Job-Toj**. Then why show your boldness and daring as you have done? Were we, the twelve lords each of whom is the master of a fortress, called by these shouts? You said quite distinctly, "Come, young men and the twelve brave men! Come and hear my words! Your supplies are all exhausted as is your water. Only crickets can be heard on the walls of your fortress as there are only nine or ten of you left with

The play "Rabinal-Achí" concerns the struggle waged between the Mayan chiefs.

very little food–perhaps a few meagre bowls of fish and beans and a few others of shrimps, macaw and other sundry dishes.

Was this not the reason for which you warned us, the lords, the leaders? Did this displace the desires of your rage and anger? Was it not there in the places called **Chi-Kotom** and **Chi-Tikiram** that the bravery of your warriors was put to the test? Now I have you here and you will pay the price for these disturbances, by the face of the earth and the sky. So, say farewell to your mountains and your valleys because we are going to end your life now. You will never again go into your valleys or climb your mountains, neither by day nor by night. Now it is necessary that you disappear from this world between the sky and the earth. Thus, I shall announce your name before my Lord, before my leader from the high walls of the great fortress. So I say to you before the sky and before the earth, may the sky and may the earth be with you, leader of the people of El Quiché.

Quiché-Achí: So be it, brave man, **Kalel-Achi**, **Rabinal-Achí**: Your words ask, "why do you make show of your courage and your valor?" Is not that your words said? In fact you were the first to provoke my Lord and my leader. This was the reason for my coming; the reason for me to leave my mountains and my valleys. From this place came the message of challenge, from here between the sky and the earth, from the walls of this fortress; it came from **Cakyug-zilic-cakocanic-tepecanic**, which are the names of the heralds and look-outs in this fortress. Were the ten loads of ordinary cocoa beans not prepared here along with the five loads of good cocoa that were sent in tribute to my lord and leader **Balam-Ahau**, **Balam-Achí** and **Balam-Quiché** which are the names of the heralds and sentinels on the walls and watch towers of my fortress? When my lord **Balam** learned of these provocations, he hungered for the death of the lord and leader of the Chacachip, the Zamanip and the **Cauk** from Rabinal in the presence of the Uxap and the Pokomanes.

"We can do wonderful things", said your lord. "Go forth and tell them that I want to sample the courage and bravery of their chief in those mountains and valleys. Let them come and take these beautiful mountains and valleys, these fertile valleys. Let them come between the sky and the earth; let them come and sow where our fruits abound, our cucumbers, our calabash, our white beans." This was the challenge, that was issued to my lord. Now I shall tell you how my lord replied, how he issued his war cry, his challenge. He said, "Go forth, my brave son! Reply and haste back because we have received the message brought to us between the sky and the earth.

"Prepare your courage, your strength, your lance and your shield and return to the mountain and the valley." This was the challenge sent by my lord, the leader of our people. Then I made busy in noting the lands where the sun sets, where night falls first, where the cold bites and where the freeze sets in, there in **Pan-Tzajakak** as it is known.

Then I drew out my lance and my shield and returned to my mountainside and my valleys. For the first time, I issued the sign of my challenges, of my battle cry in the places called **Colochic-Juyú** and **Colochic-Chaj**. From these, I issued them again in the places called **Chi-Nimché-Paraguenó** and **Cap-Rakán**. I did it a third time in the place called **Pachalib** and for a fourth time in **Xolchacoj** where I knew that the Twelve Golden Eagles and the Jaguars play the bloodied drums and deafen the earth and sky with their din. A din created by the Twelve Golden Eagles and the Jaguars which are also golden along with all their servents, their men and their women. This is how my cry started, "Come here, perverse and haughty man! You are the first man that I have been unable to defeat, leader of the Chacachip, the Zamanip and Prince of Rabinal." This is what my words said. What are you going to do, powerful lord, since I am unable to defeat you or break you? All I did was to sing my song in the face of the sky and in the face of the earth, **Kalel-Achí**, **Rabinal-Achí**. May the sky and the earth go with you!

Rabinal-Achí: Brave man, leader of the people of El Quiché! What your words really say in the face of the sky and the face of the earth, is that, "From here the messenger sent to the mountains of El Quiché and the valleys of El Quiché did in fact leave." We clearly did nothing wrong — there was nothing wrong in sending him to hear the leader **Balam**, the leader **Balam-Quiché** when the death and removal of the lord of the Chacachip and the Zamanip, the protector of Rabinal, the Uxap and the Pokomames was desired here below the sky on the face of the earth. "Let us do wonderful things to make the lord of the mountains and the valleys of El Quiché come with all his bravery. Let him come and take possession (as leader) of these beautiful mountains, these wonderful valleys. Let him come to sow them, to make furrows and plant seeds where our fruits grow, our cucumbers, our calabash and our white beans grow." That is what he said before the sky and before the earth. For this, your arrival and your challenge have all been in vain. You came with nothing more than empty threats.

May we thank the skies and the earth for your arrival among us within our walls before our fortress. For that, we accept the challenge and shall fight the leaders of Uxap and the Pokomames.

"For this, I shall send you", said my lord and leader, "so that you can call them. Go now, run to **Nim-be** where the bird drinks water before **Cholochic-Zakchún** as it is called. Do not give the Uxap and the Pokomames what they desire so much. Do not let them return to their mountains and valleys. Destroy them, wipe them out under the sky here on the earth."

This was his main message. I was not given the opportunity to withness the Uxap or the Pokomames being turned into flies, butterflies, or large and small ants whose long columns ascended the sides of the mountain called **Equempek-kanijal**. Then I looked towards them and saw before the sky and the earth, the Uxap and the Pokomames almost at the same time and my heart fell. On seeing you, my heart felt wounded and I realized that you had given way to the claims of the Uxap and the Pokomames. Then I issued my war cry and challenge to you, saying, "Ah! Brave man, leader of the people of El Quiché, why do give in to our battle against the Uxap and the Pokomames to make them return to their mountains and their valleys? Help me, oh sky! Help me, oh earth! I waited in these mountains, our mountains and our valleys for you to issue your challenge and your war cry to the Uxap and the Pokomames. Did they answer your confidence with their war cry and their challenge? Ah, leader of the Uxap and the Pokomames, listen well to what I am going to say to you below the sky on the face of the earth . . .

Act four. The Ending:

Scene: inside the palace. **Quiché-Achí** who is being guarded approaches **Job-Toj** who makes his entrance surrounded by warriors and women.

Quiché-Achi: Ah, would it suit you flautist and you drummers to play my flute and play my drum now? Play what you like — a great march or a less important match. Play my Quiché flute; play my Quiché drum! A march for my prisoner; for my captive from the mountains and my valleys! Play to move the sky and the earth! Make us bow our heads and our foreheads when we dance and when the slaves dance, here beneath the sky on the face of the earth. May they look favorably on you! Come, flautists! Come, drummers!

He dances a war dance, halting at each corner to shout his challenge. He continues:

Ah, lord **Job-Toj**! Forgive me before the sky and the earth! I have there what you lent me; what you gave me. I come to leave it at the entrance of the great walls of your fortress. Guard it, keep it within the folds of your tunic or in your coffer. You have satisfied my desires and my demands. I have affirmed this at the four corners and along the four walls of this great fortress as the supreme sign of

Mayan gods. Sacrificial offerings were made to them. 1. Chac, the rain god. 2. the sun god. 3. Ek Chuah the god of vendors. 4. Ix Chel, goddess of medicine. From the Dresden Codex.

my death and of my removal from here beneath the sky, on the face of the earth.

But... if your power is truly great on the high walls of this great fortress, your bastion, give me to the lady of the quetzal feathers of emerald green from **Tzam-kam-Carchah** (today known as San Pedro Carchá in the Verapaz uplands previously called Tezulutlán (Land of War, Guatemala) whose mouth is untouched and whose face is also untouched so that I can take her mouth and face and dance with her. I want to present her at the four corners, along the four sides of the great walls of this fortress as a supreme sign of my death and removal from here below the sky on the face of the earth. May the sky and the earth be with you lord **Job-Toj**.

Job-Toj: Brave man, leader of the people of El Quiché! Is this what you want? Is this your desire? So be it; I will grant you your request — here is the lady of the quetzal feathers, the keeper of the bird with the beautiful emerald green feathers from **Tzam-kam-Carchah**, the lady whose mouth is untouched and whose face is untouched. I give her to you brave man as a supreme sign of your death! Slaves! Bring the lady of the quetzal feathers and deliver her unto this brave man as he desires as the supreme sign of his death here beneath the sky on the face of the earth!

The slaves bring the mistress of the green feathers and present her to **Quiché-Achí**, saying:

Here she is, brave man, leader of the people of El Quiché. We give you your desire as you requested. Take care and do not insult her, do not wound her as she is the mistress of the quetzal plumes. Only allow yourself to be seen dancing with her before the high walls of the great fortress.

Quiché-Achí greets the young girl and she begins to dance keeping her eyes on his face. He follows her, doing likewise. When they arrive before **Job-Toj**, he stops and says:

Quiché-Achí: Lord **Job-Toj**, forgive me before the sky and before the earth! Here is she who was given to me as a companion. I went to show her and dance with her round the four corners, along the four sides and before the high walls of the great fortress. My words also say, "Give me or lend me the twelve Golden Eagles and the twelve Golden Jaguars who I always met at night and during the day with arms in their hands. Let me go and jibe them with the point of my lance and test the strength of my shield at the four corners, along the four sides just as a sign of my death and my removal from here beneath the sky on the earth. May the sky and the earth be with you, Lord **Job-Toj**!

Job-Toj: Brave man, leader of the people of El Quiché! Your words request me to lend you the twelve Golden Eagles and the twelve Golden Jaguars. This is what you asked for and I give my consent — I will lend you what you wish; what you asked for before me. Go, my eagles! Go, my jaguars! Let this brave man go with you to test the point of his lance and the strength of his shield.

Quiché-Achí goes with the eagles and the jaguars and they dance a war dance around the stage. When the dance is finished, they turn to **Job-Toj**:

Quiché-Achí: Lord **Job-Toj**, forgive me before the sky and the earth! My words are asking you to grant me twenty days, thirteen times and twenty nights, thirteen times so that I can say farewell to my mountains and to my valleys where I used to roam. Let me go to the four corners and the four sides of my land to look for food and sustenance.

Silence. **Quiché-Achí** quickly disappears from the stage and returns. He addresses the twelve eagles and the twelve jaguars:

Quiché-Achi: Oh, eagles! Oh, jaguars! He has left, you thought. He has gone, you said. I neither left nor went. I merely went to say farewell to my mountains and my valleys where I used to look for and find my sustenance.

Help me, oh sky! Help me, oh earth! It is true that I must die and disappear from here beneath the sky on the face of

A human sacrifice is depicted on this gold disc found in the sacred cenote at Chichén Itzá, Yucatán, Mexico.

the earth. Oh, my golden metal! Oh, the point of my lance! Oh, the hardness of my shield and my **yaqui** mace (this is a reference to the Mexican origins of those tribes who migrated to El Quiché in Guatemala with the Toltecs.) Oh, my **yaqui** axe, my garlands, my sandals. Go to our mountains and our valleys! Take this news to my lord and leader!

These are the words of my lord, "It is a long time now since your bravery and your courage looked for our food!" That is what he said. I am not just saying this because I am awaiting my death and my removal. Help me, oh earth at my moment of death when I shall disappear from here beneath the sky from the face of the earth. I can no longer turn myself into a squirrel or a bird dying on the branch of a tree! Oh, eagles! Oh, jaguars! Come and do your duty and the task which is expected of you with your sharp teeth and your claws. May you destroy me quickly since I have been a brave man who came from the mountains and the valleys. May the sky and the earth be with me! Oh, eagles! Oh, jaguars!

The eagles and the jaguars spring on **Quiché-Achi**. They spread him on the altar and tear out his heart with blades of obsidian and flint. They all dance to a monotonous sound which gradually dies away. The play ends.

Outstanding Examples of Mayan Culture

A selection compiled by Sylvannus G. Morley

The oldest city: Tikal. The largest: Tikal. Where the study of astronomy was most developed: Copán. Where stone sculpting reached its finest expression: Piedras Negras. Where molding in stucco reached its most advanced levels: Palenque.

Where the finest examples of woods carvings are: Tikal. The finest example of architecture: Uxmal. The holiest city of the New Empire: Chichén Itzá. Completely walled (known) cities: Mayapán, Tulum and Becam. The city with the largest ball court: Chichén Itzá. The city with the oldest astronomical observatory: Uaxactún.

Where the most beautiful painted ceramics have been founds: Uaxactún. The city with the greatest number of stone sculpted lintels: Yaxchilán (59). The city with the most steles: Calakmul (103 of which 79 are sculpted and 24 are smooth). Where the oldest earthenware pot was found (Mammón): Uaxactún. Where the finest articles made of flint were recovered: Quriguá.

The oldest construction: the stucco covered pyramid, number E-VII Sub. at Uaxactún. The most beautiful building: the Governor's House at Uxmal. The highest building: Temple IV or Temple of the Great Jaguar at Tikal (70 meters). The largest structure: the Acropolis at Copán. The oldest dated object: the jade plaque of Leyden (from Guatemala), date 320 B.C. The oldest, dated stone sculpture: stele 9 at Uaxactún, dated 388 A.D., Early Classic Period.

The earliest indication of the twenty year period known as **El Katún**: on steles 18 and 19 at Uaxactún, 357 A.D., Early Classic Period. The earliest indication of the ten year periods known as **lahuntunes**: stele 5 in Balakbal, 406 A.D. The earliest indication of the five year periods known as **hotunes**: stele 25 at Piedras Negras, 608 A.D., beginning of the Late Classic Period.

The largest block of stone removed from a quarry: stele E. at Quiriguá, 10.67 meters tall, 65 tonnes weight. The most beautiful example of stone sculpture: wall panel number 3 in structure 0-13 at Piedras Negras. The most beautiful example of wood engraving: the lintel of the shrine in the Temple of the Great Jaguar or Temple IV at Tikal worked in sapodilla plum wood. It is in good condition.

The finest example of modeling in stucco: the Temple of the Beautiful Relief at Palenque. The prototype of lintels carved from stone: Lintel 24 of structure 23 at Yaxchilán.

The most important individual object discovered in the Mayan world: the Throne of the Red Jaguar which is inlaid with seventy-three discs of jade, below the Castle at Chichén Itzá.

The most beautiful example of sculpted low-reliefs: the panel of the Temple of the Cross at Palenque. The oldest mural painting: the back wall of the chamber of structure B-XIII at Uaxactún. The most interesting wall mural: the "Fishing Village" in the Temple of the Warriors at Chichén Itzá. (Sylvannus G. Morley died shortly after the discovery of the murals at Bonampak which are undoubtedly the most beautiful and important remains of Mayan painting.)

The most beautiful jade piece: the plaque at San Juan Teotihuacán. The largest jade piece: a seated human statuette found under the steps of temple A-XVIII at Uaxactún.

The largest piece of rough jade found: a block which was discovered under a staircase in Kaminal-Juyú which weighed ninety kilograms. The only piece of metal to be found in a city of the Old Empire: a pair of (hollow) gold. legs found under stele H. at Copán.

The largest archaeological dig in the world: the Acropolis at Copán which measures 300 meters long and 35 meters high and was uncovered by the river Copán.

The most important mathematical monument: stele 10 at Tikal. The number of days recorded on it comprise eight orders of units or 1 841.641 600 days of 5.047 277 years. The longest hieroglyphic inscription: the staircase of Temple 26 at Copán.

The most beautiful hieroglyphics carved on stone: the inscription on stele F. at Quriguá. The hieroglyphic inscription with the most errors: stele E. at Quriguá — it has four mistakes. The most complicated and ornate hierogyphics: the inscription on zoomorph B. at Quiriguá which has hieroglyphs of whole figures. The hieroglyphic inscription with the greatest number of initial series: the hieroglyphic scale leading to Temple 26 at Copán which has eighteen initial series.

The oldest use of numerals in leader form: stele 15 at Copán, 524 A.D. The monument with the greatest number of initial series: stele 1 at Cobá. (Four inital series.) The most modern monuments of the Classic Period: stele 12 at Uaxactún, stele 10 at Xultún and stele 1 at Xamantún. Article with the most recent date of the Classic Period: a jade pendant from Dzibanché, 909 A.D., Late Classic Period, beginning of the Post-classic Period.

Archaeological sites and seats of culture mentioned in the text.

MEXICO

Acanceh
Becam
Bonampak
Calakmul
Chichén-Itzá
Chincultik
Comalcalco
Cobá
Dzibanché
El Bellote
Etzná
Hochob
Izamal
Jaina
Jonuta
Kabah
Kohunlich
Maní
Mayapán
Nocuchic
Palenque
Santa Rosa Xtampak
Sayil
Tulum
Uxmal
Xamantún
Xel-Ha
Yaxchilán

GUATEMALA

Altar de Sacrificios
Balakbal
Cancúen
Chamá
Chunhuitz
El Naranjo
Holmul
Kaminal Juyú
La Honradez
Mixco Viejo
Naachtún
Nakum
Nebaj
Piedras Negras
Quiriguá
San Clemente
Santa Lucia Cotzumalguapa (Cultural Areas)
San Agustín Acasahuastlán
Seibal
Tayasal
Tikal
Totonicapán (Cultural Areas)
Uaxactún
Xultún
Yaxhá
Zaculeu

BELIZE

Benque Viejo
Corozal
Lubaantún
Pusilhá
Santa Rita
Xinantunich

HONDURAS

Copán
Valle de Ulúa (Cultural Areas)

Archaeologist, researchers and others mentioned in the text

ALVARADO, PEDRO DE (1485-1541) Hernán Cortés' deputy during the Conquest. Conqueror of Guatemala.

BLOM, FRANZ (1893-1963) Danish born researcher and explorer. Expert on the ruins at Palenque.

BRASSEUR DE BOURBURG, ETIENNE CHARLES (1814-1874) French priest and Mayan expert. He published the first edition of the **Popol Vuh** in French in Paris in 1861.

COLUMBUS CHRISTOPHER (1451?-1506) Navigator from Genova. Discovered the New World while in the employment of the Catholic Monarchs of Spain.

CORTES, HERNAN (1485-1547) Conqueror of Mexico. Author of the famous letters sent to Emperor Charles V of Spain.

DIAZ DEL CASTILLO, BERNAL (1492-1581) Spanish soldier and chronicler of the Conquest of Mexico.

FUENTES Y GUZMAN, FRANCISCO DE (1643-1700) Captain and historian of Spanish parents but born in Guatemala.

GIRARD, RAFAEL (1901-) Anthropologist and ethnologist of Swiss-French origin.

LANDA, DIEGO DE (1524-1579) Spanish cleric and historian. After the Conquest, he became the first Bishop of the Yucatán.

LAS CASAS, BARTOLOME DE (1474-1566) Cleric and Bishop from Spain. Protector of the Indians.

LIZANA, BERNARDO DE (—) Spanish historian. Author of several books on Mexico published during the seventeenth century.

LOPEZ DE COGOLLUDO, DIEGO (—) Spanish author of "A History of the Yucatán" published in Madrid in 1688.

MEDIZ BOLIO, ANTONIO (1884-1957) Writer, poet and Mayan expert from the Yucatán.

MORLEY, SYLVANNUS G. (1883-1948) American archaeologist linguist and researcher. One of the leading Mayan experts of all time.

REMESAL, ANTONIO DE (—) Spanish cleric of the sixteenth century. Author of "A History of Chiapas and Guatemala".

REYNAUD, GEORGES (—) Mayan expert and linguist from France.

SCHULTZE-JENA, LEONHARDT (1872-1955) German anthropologist and linguist.

SAHAGUN, BERNARDINO DE (1500?-1590) Spanish cleric and historian. Author of "A General History of New Spain".

SAMAYOA CHINCHILLA, CARLOS (1898-) Director of the Institute of Anthropology and History of Guatemala. Author of several books of short stories and books on archaeology.

THOMPSON, S. ERIC J. (1898-1976) English archaeologist who explored the world of the Mayans for twenty years. Wrote several books and articles of great importance about Mayan culture.

TORQUEMADA, JUAN DE (1557 or 1565-1624) Spanish cleric and historian.

TOZZER, ALFRED (1877-1954) Archaeologist from the Peabody Museum and Harvard University, USA.

WESTHEIM, PAUL (1885-1963) Art critic born in Bolivia. Wrote "The Ancient Art of Mexico".

XIMENEZ, FRANCISCO (1666-1722) Spanish cleric who made the first translation into Spanish of the **Popol Vuh** in 1722.

Printed in:
Edicupes, S.A.
Av. San Lorenzo 251
Col. San Nicolás Tolentino
09850 México, D.F.
1000 Copies
Mexico City, August, 1991